GOD OF OUR FATHERS

A Black Legacy of Miracles, Signs and Wonders

Kesean Joseph

Copyright © 2021

First Edition

All rights reserved. No part of this publication may be reproduced or transmitted in any form or by any means, electronic or mechanical, including photocopy, recording, or any information storage retrieval system, without permission in writing from the copyright owner.

GOD OF OUR FATHERS

A Black Legacy of Miracles, Signs and Wonders

Kesean Joseph

First Edition

TABLE OF CONTENTS

Dedication 4

Foreword 5

Preface 9

Arturo Skinner 14

Johnnie Washington 62

Prophet Mosley 98

Epilogue 130

DEDICATION

I dedicate this book to the next generation of five-fold ministry gifts. I have conducted this research and composed this book with you in mind. My prayer is that this book will activate something afresh in you. I pray that we will learn from the good and bad of the generations before us and continue to expand God's Kingdom in new and innovative ways.

FOREWORD BY: HEZEKIAH X. WALKER

Legacy and history has always been important to God. Throughout the Scriptures, he constantly revealed himself as the God of Abraham, Isaac and Jacob.

As I write this foreword, I am reminded of Genesis 26:18 where the Bible says " And Isaac dug again the wells of water which they had dug in the days of Abraham his father, for the Philistines had stopped them up after the death of Abraham. He called them by the names which his father had called them."

This verse alone is loaded with principles for revival. I fear that many people in this current generation are "reinventing the wheel" when they don't need to. Isaac did not need to dig a brand new well for himself. There were multiple wells available to him that he needed to rediscover and uncover again. Kesean is a historian in his own right. He comes from a rich ministry legacy himself. He has undertaken an honorable task with this book. Rather than creating something that already existed, he has shown us the map where the wells are for us to re-dig again. New things are always great, but learning history will ensure that you are doing something brand new and not repeating what has already been done by our Forefathers. I have been greatly influenced by each of these men of God mentioned in this book.

Apostle Arturo Skinner was a household name in the 1960s and 70s, especially in New York City. He was known for his powerful ministry of healing and deliverance. "Deliverance" was a force to be reckoned with. I remember his church purchased the former Kismet Theatre on Dekalb and Tompkins. Another great evangelist, Mother Mattie B. Poole out of Chicago was located on Hart Street not too far from him. Mother Poole also flowed heavily in gifts of healing. Her husband planted a church in Brooklyn that she pastored while not in Chicago. She and Apostle Skinner shook the region with the power of God. After Mother Poole passed, many of her members came over to Bibleway Church where I was. After Apostle Skinner passed away, many of his members went over to Apostle Johnnie Washington's church.

Apostle Washington was my greatest influence. Although many people know me for my music, my passion was really for ministry. The word "Crusade" in "Love Fellowship Crusade Choir" is an homage to Apostle Washington because he used and embodied that word in his ministry. I can remember visiting his church and it being packed every

Sunday. His choir stood in black and white and sang until the anointing of God was made manifest. I tried to recreate that same image and discipline with Love Fellowship. I was terrified of him because his preaching was so direct and sobering. When I finally did meet him he asked me "What church do you come from?" "Bibleway Temple", I replied. "Oh, the waterbug church" he responded jokingly. "They want to get you in the water as soon as you come in the door!" To hear him laugh, smile and express his sense of humor was so surprising to me. Apostle Washington was such a kind man but his ministry was strikingly powerful. He was not afraid to confront error, be it in person or on the radio. His passing was shocking to the whole city. I was determined to keep his legacy of deliverance alive.

In the 1980s I attended church in Bridgeport at Prayer Tabernacle with Bishop Kenneth Moales. It is there that I discovered the ministry of Prophet Brian Mosley. Prophet Mosley was a highly revered name in Connecticut. I remember when he first started coming to New York and New Jersey. His meeting was the first time I had ever witnessed a miracle. He was in revival at Bishop Loughlin High School auditorium. A woman came with a foot that was terribly swollen and almost disfigured.

Mosley began to pray and I watched her leg shrink down to size right there before my very eyes. The whole audience erupted in praise! I remember him pastoring in Newark and then his transition into full-time itinerant ministry. Prophet Mosley's contribution to the prophetic ministry cannot be understated.

I encourage you, don't think of this book as an old relic. This book is a well that must be uncovered and revealed. We do well and save time when we revive the works of our Fathers. It also gives us more time to blaze our own trail and bring fresh contribution to the wealth of the anointing in the Body of Christ.

Lastly, don't just focus on the men. Don't get lost on their methods and style. Focus on the God of those men. What attributes of God do we see in their ministry? What parts of the Scripture did they embody? Let us honor and worship the God of our Fathers.

PREFACE

The 21st century brought an explosion of Pentecostal-Charismatic Christianity in the United States. We would be surprised to find that a few decades ago, this would have been unheard of. Pentecostals were widely shunned. Pentecostalism was considered a silly, unkempt, uneducated, and shameful denomination. The name "Holy Roller" was anything but a badge of honor. Interestingly enough, the Pentecostal denomination was one of few denominations founded and established by black people. While Baptist and Methodist traditions already existed, Pentecostalism was established and expanded by William Seymour, a black man. Coincidentally, many of the accusations laid upon the early Pentecostals were those laid on black people as well: uneducated, unkempt, emotional, and so on. Pentecostalism and its elements reside in the hearts of black people from all walks of life. Its narrative theology is the fruit of our storytelling abilities. Its spontaneity a fruit of the creativity of our ancestors. Its dynamic nature, the fruit of our fiery roots.

That being said, one cannot discuss Pentecostal history and the ministry of the supernatural without discussing the contribution of the many black men and women of God. I am a huge fan of the God's Generals book series. Dr. Roberts Liardon does a masterful job of documenting the life and ministry of many of God's supernatural leaders. After reading so many books and watching so many videos, I determined that there must be a book discussing signs and wonders from the black generals as well. I do not believe they were excluded purposefully. Perhaps they were omitted because of a lack of information about their lives. In fact, during the "heyday" of the healing evangelists such as Oral Roberts, Jack Coe, and A.A. Allen, there were no black ministers with noted healing ministries like them. I have already mentioned William Seymour, the progenitor of modern Pentecostalism. I also cannot start this story without mentioning Bishop Charles Harrison Mason, founder of the Church of God in Christ. Bishop Mason continued the legacy of Seymour by blending his powerful ministry of the Spirit with an ability to organize churches into the largest African-American denomination in the world. Mason was known for his strong prayer and intercessory ministry. But as Dr. Brian Mosley stated "Men like Mason were rare." Meaning, men who yielded themselves to the supernatural were rare. Men embraced preaching but the more mystical elements were considered feminine in the black church. Bishop Mason's death in 1961 could signal the ending of an era in the realm of signs and wonders in the black church.

So what caused the explosion of spiritual gifts that we see today with both men and women in the black church? The better question is who caused it? Apostle Arturo Skinner was the first from the black community to achieve notoriety through supernatural ministry, which is why he was considered the "black Oral Roberts." He would go on to pioneer a move of the Spirit in the urban community that would produce many other black ministers who walked in supernatural ministry, namely: Johnny Washington and Brian Mosley.

The labor of these figures in the ministry of the Spirit cannot be ignored. They must be told to the next generation. The Scriptures unapologetically testify of the successes, failures, and flaws of its great characters. The Apostle Paul says Scripture does this that we might learn from their mistakes (1 Cor. 10:11). I would also add that we might follow in their successes. My prayer is that we do not try to re-invent the wheel but build on the foundation that has been laid.

There are a few things to be noted of all three figures mentioned above. Each of them contributed to the Body of Christ in a way that has affected generations. All three of these figures are from the Northeast.

Two are from New York City and one from Connecticut, just a few miles away. There is much to be said of the black presence in the Northeast. From the Great Migration to the Harlem Renaissance, what happened in the North affected the whole black population and ultimately, the nation. The Northern part of the country seemed to set the rhythm that the African American population moves to. From these cities, these three men affected the nucleus of the black population and transformed the black church experience nationally. They caused people to come from around the country and later take the same experiences back to various parts of the country, from Pennsylvania to Florida to North Carolina and even abroad.

All three of these men were unmarried, one for the majority of his ministry. They devoted themselves completely to the service of God and to serving the Body of Christ. Jesus said that those who are unmarried are a foretaste of the Kingdom of God (Matt. 19:10-12). All of these men of God overcame parental issues, left their comfort zones, renounced sin and lived consecrated to ministering to the Body of Christ. They mentored, cared, covered, and loved intensely. Their passion for the lost fueled their drive whether it was in a tent in the most dangerous part of a city or in a palace before royalty. There are many challenges to providing a history of these individuals. First, there is not much official documentation or scholarly articles on these figures. In my research, I had to gather information from books, souvenir journals, and miscellaneous items in order to try to reconstruct their lives and ministries. My desire is that this reading provides an objective and yet powerful approach to these men of God's lives and that they will receive the respect and honor they are due.

ARTURO SKINNER

The ministry of the apostle has always been one of controversy in the modern church. The question is, "Are apostles for today?" "What is an apostle?" "What makes someone an apostle?" These questions have varying beliefs, even in the Pentecostal church. The last few years have seen a surge in the popularity through what's called the New Apostolic Reformation. This movement began in the 1990s and affirms that there are apostles today who are to be known by their signs and wonders. This movement comes with the rejection of the title of "Bishop" within their leaders and instead emphasizes the importance of revelation and demonstration regarding the office of an apostle. A casual scan of social media and ministry advertisements will show the surging popularity of the title "Apostle." To our surprise though, the office of apostle did not simply make its re-introduction in the 1990s with C. Peter Wagner. The office of apostleship made a noted reappearance with its revelation and demonstration in the 1960s with a man of God named Arturo Skinner.

EARLY LIFE

Arthur Alfred Skinner was born December 15, 1924, to Ethel and James Skinner in Brooklyn, New York. He is the third of four sons born to his Barbados-native parents. Ethel Skinner was a devout Christian, attending a local Church of the Nazarene where they taught holiness and sanctified lifestyles. James Skinner Sr. left the family and returned to Barbados, taking two brothers with him. This caused Arturo to assume leadership of his family by searching for gainful employment to assist his mother. He was a natural leader.

New York City has always been a melting pot of many racial backgrounds. It's central location and nearness to Ellis Island, an immigration checkpoint, made it the prime locale for racial diversity. This multi-ethnic context would help shape young Arthur into the man of God he would be. Brooklyn housed a considerable Jewish population during the time of young Arthur's childhood. He befriended many Jewish children where he learned Yiddish and Hebrew. From his youth, Skinner showed an uncanny ability to adapt, thrive in any environment, and connect with people from different backgrounds. Young Arthur used his newfound language skills to be a translator at the local welfare department.

The Jewish kids began to call him "Arturo," a transliteration of the name Arthur. Thereafter, he soon changed his name legally to "Arturo."

At the same time, Arturo was also developing his artistic side through dancing. He developed a love for tap dancing and the entertainment world at large. He soon found himself on the stage at various large theatres in New York City performing through dancing. His exuberant personality kept him at the center of attention through tap dancing, acting, and hosting shows. Along with this notoriety came its own challenges. Much of Arturo's popularity was a combination of his skilled dancing with his young age. As he grew into adulthood, Arturo developed an alcohol addiction and heroin habit that became hard to shake. At the same time, Arturo's popularity began to wane as his maturity was not as attractive as his youthfulness. As the phone stopped ringing, his addiction continued to worsen. To quote him from one of his sermons, "By the age of twelve years, I was dancing in night clubs…and at 27, I had become an alcoholic. I went from drinking whiskey to taking dope." Then in September of 1952, Arturo's beloved mother passed away suddenly.

CALL TO MINISTRY

This tragic event launched him into a major depression in which he felt his only option was to take his own life. He planned to jump in front of a train. Before he could do so, Arturo said he heard a voice saying, "If you but turn around, I'll save your soul, heal your body, and give you a deliverance ministry." The latter statement would burn a permanent mark in Arturo's heart and go on to be the earmark of his ministry. What deliverance would look like for this 28-year-old entertainer would be a very humbling, deconstructing, but transforming experience.

Arturo gave away everything in his house and set his eyes on Hartford, Connecticut for his "Burning Bush" experience where he would consecrate himself, encounter God, and forsake his former life. Arturo was determined to drop his drug and alcohol habit without formal medical assistance. He would rely totally on God to set him free from his addiction supernaturally. Consequently, he would experience the deliverance that he would also bring to thousands afterward. For over a month in a hotel, Arturo devoted himself to ardent prayer and fasting as he weaned himself off his habit. James Blocker writes: "During those tumultuous days, according to Skinner, he fasted and prayed as God dealt with him in dreams and visions."² After 56 days in Connecticut, he returned to New York with a burden to preach the Gospel and the message of deliverance. Determined to learn all that he could about the Scriptures, he enrolled in Bethel Bible Institute in Jamaica, Queens under Bishop Roderick Caesar. He became a member of Bethel's church and received the Baptism in the Holy Ghost under Bishop Caesar also. Completing his studies, he was ordained an evangelist by their church and set out to carry out his ministry.

MOVES OF THE SPIRIT

There were various Pentecostal revival movements throughout the 20th century. The initial and largest movement was the Azusa Movement from 1906-1922. However, after World War II there was another revival called The Latter Rain Movement from 1948 until the late 1950s. The Latter Rain movement introduced or restored many concepts such as laying on of hands for blessing or impartation and speaking in tongues publicly in praise to God.

Whereas tongues were always present in Pentecostal churches after a person received the Holy Spirit, the only other time you heard tongues publicly was when they were being interpreted. The laying on of hands was mainly for the healing of the sick, baptism in the Holy Spirit, and ordination. But in this movement, the ministers laid hands spontaneously and people were often slain in the spirit or received spiritual gifts. Historian Vinson Synan wrote, "What was different [about Latter Rain] was the practice of imparting specific gifts of the Holy Spirit by the 'laying on of hands', frequent cases of mass singing in tongues and detailed personal prophecies directing individuals to make life changing decisions."[3] Lastly, The Latter Rain Movement restored the use of all the fivefold ministry titles including "Apostle" and "Prophet." Although the movement waned, these elements would remain in Pentecostal-Charismatic churches permanently.

At the same time, another movement called the Voice of Healing was equally stirring the nation. Evangelists like William Branham, Oral Roberts, A.A. Allen, Kenneth Hagin, and Jack Coe were at the forefront of this movement moving specifically in the gift of healing and miracles. Their tents would often be crowded with sick and afflicted people. The attendees would be exhilarated by watching dozens of people be healed miraculously before their very eyes.

Branham also operated in a heavy gift of word of knowledge in which he could reveal secrets of a person's condition and life. Oral Roberts specialized in a twofold ministry of physical healing and spiritual deliverance through the laying on of hands. He would lay hands on hundreds of people and watch many of them be healed before an audience of thousands in his tent.

In the beginning of his evangelistic ministry, Evangelist Arturo would visit the tents of many of these evangelists, especially Oral Roberts. The Voice of Healing evangelists even had a monthly magazine named after themselves which circulated to thousands, along with radio and television appearances. But it should be noted that none of the prominent Voice of Healing evangelists were black. Although many of them ministered to black people, there was a lack of black presence in the Voice of Healing revival's forefront. At the time of this revival, many of the prominent black Pentecostal leaders such as Bishops R.C. Lawson, F.D. Washington, GT Haywood, and CH Mason were given mainly to prayer and powerful preaching. Although there were certainly supernatural elements, there was no black preacher flowing in the supernatural at the level and popularity of the Voice of Healing evangelists. Evangelist

Skinner noticed this and prayed to God about it. According to Blocker, "Skinner maintained that God spoke to him and said if a black man would pay the price, then He would use him. According to Skinner, he vowed that he would be one black man that would 'pay the price.'"[4]

In 1956, Evangelist Skinner began leading prayer meetings in someone's home in Newark, New Jersey. Dr. Clarence Taylor, church historian, wrote, "Despite similarities, between Deliverance Evangelistic and other Holiness Pentecostal groups, the major emphasis and attraction of Skinner's group was divine healing."[5] Word began to spread, and his following began to build. In 1957, he established the Newark Deliverance Evangelistic Center. His meetings were often filled to capacity and his ministry was accompanied with exponential growth. Simultaneously, he was hosting "Deliverance Rallies" in Brooklyn, New York that were filled to capacity as well. Soon thereafter, they purchased a former theatre and named it the Brooklyn Deliverance Evangelistic Center with a sanctuary, executive suite, bookstore, photography studio, and more. The Brooklyn center became the public relations center for the movement. The message of "Deliverance" was spreading quickly in the New York Metropolitan area.

THE APOSTLE

As mentioned above, the most debated office in the church is the office of apostle. The debates that we see raging today are hardly new. They even happened in 1963. On April 28, Evangelist Skinner was consecrated Apostle Arturo Skinner. In contrast, most denominations during this time, such as COGIC, PAW, and other organizations, used Bishop as their "highest" title in the black church. Some Pentecostal churches affirmed that Bishops are the successors to the apostles and lean on Church history such as the writings of Ignatius to affirm so.[6] Other Pentecostal churches flat out rejected the notion of "present day apostles and prophets" as heretical and the fruit of "wrestlings and distortions of Scripture."[7] The Biblical ambiguity behind this specific title added to the disputes. Whereas the office of bishop, elder, and deacon are explained and the requirements are laid out clearly in the New Testament, the term "apostle" is not specified nor is it as self-explanatory as the title of "teacher." What makes someone an apostle? What are its qualifications? What is the difference between an "apostle" and a "bishop"? All of these questions came up during the time of this consecration with little to no sufficient answers given. Many adherents to the apostolic office have since developed in-depth explanations of the office. Teachers that affirm apostleship believe that an apostle is a "sent one" or "one with a direct commission from God to complete an assignment."

In the world during Jesus' day, apostles functioned in a similar fashion to the ancient envoys in Greco-Roman culture. Their responsibility was to represent and influence the culture of a region by introducing the kingdom or nation that they represented.[8] This definition complements the teaching of the Church of God in Christ who believed the ministry of apostleship to be representative of a special authority. Their manual states, "New Testament apostleship lay then in the missionary calling implied in the name, and that all devoted to this vocation and who could prove by the issues of their labors that God's spirit was working through them."[9] By this definition, that is exactly what Apostle Skinner did and continued to do for the years to follow. He established a network of churches that were spread around the nation in the name of "Deliverance."

CONSECRATION: A DAY IN DELIVERANCE

During its heyday, the Deliverance churches were a sight to

behold! At its peak in the early 1970s, the Deliverance churches of Brooklyn, Newark, and Philadelphia boasted of a combined local membership of 25,000 people. They also boasted of a 500-voice choir and 50-piece orchestra in their church. Choir members often could be identified by their black and white suits for men, black skirt and white top for women, and their "Christ is the Answer" button pin. They would flood the streets with a sea of black and white as they were on their way to worship or hosting an outdoor crusade. The Newark church was the headquarters for the mission. Here is where they held the main and high church services. The Brooklyn Church became the executive offices, home to special events, crusades, and regular services. Most of the workers were stationed at the Brooklyn church in their executive offices that included a photo studio, a recording studio, and a mailing center. The church itself was heavily centered on prayer. It is reported that Apostle Skinner would pay certain saints to live at the Newark church and pray there continually. Every Tuesday they held a prayer and anointing service where everyone present was anointed with oil—no matter the size of the crowd. The church fasted every Tuesday and oftentimes the church was called into 40 Days of Consecration.

Apostle Skinner stood out by hosting his services at 3:00 p.m. on Sundays. According to his biographer, "The strategy was that those persons connected with this evangelistic group that were members of other churches…could attend their own church services and still be present at the Deliverance services."[10] Although some attendants were members elsewhere, a large portion of the membership was saved from out of the world. Skinner's ministry was largely evangelistic. They hosted many crusades, rallies, and outreach events to minister to the lost. Deliverance had multiple witnessing teams that circulated through the city ministering to those on the streets about the Gospel of Jesus Christ. There was a large sign in the church that read, "10 Million Soul Crusade." This highlighted Skinner's driving passion to reach at least 10 million souls with the Gospel message. This was done through preaching, but largely through demonstration of miracles, signs, and wonders.

In his book 9 Gifts of the Spirit, he writes, "Miracles draw the attention of unbelievers. Miracles strengthen the faith of believers…It is going to take the supernatural miracle power of God to reach the unreached masses for Christ…except some people see or experience a miracle, they will never believe" (Skinner 26-27). Apostle Skinner was not known for his preaching skill and often did not preach lengthy sermons. But instead, his sermons were of a prophetic nature as he often opened with, "God has been speaking to me…" before delivering his message. This gave the message added authority and urgency as a "rhema" word from God. This became such a trademark of his that his ministers who often came out of his church would repeat the same thing as a formality, whether they believe God spoke with them or not!

The Deliverance Churches hosted a conference called the "World Deliverance Convention" annually in various venues and auditoriums. The largest of which was Madison Square Garden for four days in 1971. Over 25,000 people attended the meetings with the altar being filled nightly with people dedicating their lives to God. This was largely unheard of for a Pentecostal church to accomplish at this time and Skinner continued to break barriers and challenge stereotypes through "Deliverance."

Sermons were often short, but he took his time to minister through the supernatural. Skinner operated largely through word of knowledge and discernment of spirits. Sometimes he would wait until he finished preaching, but often times it was mid-sermon. He would walk the aisle of the Church and as he was walking, he would state: "I feel there is someone on this row dealing with...step out into the aisle if that's you." He would feel the pain or have a strong impression to pray for something and then minister to that person. One member recalled, "They would bring people to the church from the hospital and many of them would never go back to the hospital because they would be healed. They would be able to go home with their family."[11]

Skinner explained his Apostolic theology in his book 9 Gifts of the Spirit, "Healing is the creating of that which was not or recreating of that which was destroyed. It is life triumphing over death."[12] Although it was often spontaneous, the laying on of hands was a major method of ministering healing, deliverance, and blessing. The church believed that the laying on of hands was a point of contact and often referred to James 5:14. "The healer was said to be in direct communication with God, practiced the laying on of hands...and called on God in an assertive voice to heal the invalid. As proof of his power, Skinner decorated the walls of his church with the wheelchairs, canes, and crutches of the people."[13]

This power was not just reserved for Apostle Skinner though. All the members of the Church were encouraged to use spiritual gifts in witnessing to the lost and bound. This was seen as an increase of power and efficiency rather than leaving all the ministry to Apostle Skinner. Through this "Deliverance would take the land."

The elaborate and demonstrative nature of the Deliverance ministry often stirred controversy with other Pentecostal ministries. Historian Vinson Synan writes, "Deliverance ministries were touted as being more in touch with the power of God than the average black Pentecostal congregations. Most of these ministries reinforced the sanctified church identity with their emphasis on consecration, demonstrative expressions, jubilance, and religious dancing. By 1956, Arturo Skinner was a key figure"14 (Synan 2001). Contemporaries included Mother Mattie B. Poole who had planted a church, Bethlehem Healing Temple, nearby Skinner in Brooklyn. Poole was also known for a profound healing ministry. Parallel elements of his ministry could be seen in fellow laborers such as Apostle Richard Henton of Chicago, Charles O. Miles of Michigan, and Bishop Harold J. Benjamin of Pennsylvania. Apostle Skinner unknowingly branded a new genre of Pentecostalism, one that appealed to the urban community. Despite the criticisms, the results of this ministry could not be denied. Every month, the Deliverance Voice magazine was loaded with testimonies of documented miracles and healings that took place under Apostle Skinner's ministry. Mrs. Lillian Graver stated: "I came to Reverend Skinner for prayer six years ago…the doctor gave me six months to live. Reverend Skinner prayed the prayer of faith and God worked a miracle and healed the cancer."[15]

Mrs. Alma Haley in Rocky Mount, North Carolina testified, "All my life I was blind. Reverend Skinner asked me to remain for special prayer. As he said, 'You blind demon, I rebuke you in the name of Jesus!' I felt something—the power of God from the crown of my head to the sole of my feet. When I opened my eyes, I could see for the first time in my life. I walked back to my seat unaided by anyone. Praise God for the supernatural miracle in my life."[16] Many of the miracles, signs, and wonders that occurred in the ministry were answers to social ills that were common in the black and brown communities at this time. Divine healing was God's answer to the lack of health care and medical assistance in the ghettos. The young man who survived multiple gunshot wounds and miraculously recovered testified to God's providence in the presence of violence and gang activity in the community. In fact, many gang members got saved and became members of "Deliverance" under his ministry. There were equally as many former drug addicts who were able to kick the habit through prayer and discipleship rather than relying on rehabilitation programs. To aid him in his ministry to the sick, he often sent out cloths that he prayed over as a point of contact for the sick and afflicted. Apostle Skinner also conducted revivals across the country to spread the message of "Deliverance."

Although largely focused on the supernatural, Apostle Skinner strongly rejected any sectarian or elitist views. "Is the Holy Ghost only for those who come under the banner of Deliverance? By no means! No matter what your denominational preference, when the Holy Ghost is fully come into your life, your ministry is that of Deliverance."[17]

Deliverance Voice

REACHING THE UNREACHED MASSES WITH THE MESSAGE OF JESUS CHRIST! NOT TO BE SOLD!

"The Spirit of the Lord is upon me, because he hath anointed me to preach the gospel to the poor; he hath sent me to heal the brokenhearted, to preach deliverance to the captives, and recovering of sight to the blind, to set at liberty them that are bruised to preach the acceptable year of the Lord." —St. Luke 4:18, 19

| CIRCULATION: 200,000 | JANUARY • FEBRUARY 1975 | VOLUME 9 • NUMBER 1 |

And these signs shall follow them that believe; In my name shall they cast out devils; they shall speak with new tongues; They shall take up serpents; and if they drink any deadly thing, it shall not hurt them;

THEY SHALL LAY HANDS ON THE SICK AND THEY SHALL RECOVER. St. Mark 16: 17, 18

THESE ARE THE HANDS OF GOD'S APOSTLE...

WE believe...

1. In the verbal inspiration of the Bible.
2. In one God eternally existing in three persons; namely the Father, Son, and Holy Ghost.
3. That Jesus Christ is the only begotten Son of the Father, conceived of the Holy Ghost, and born of the virgin Mary. That Jesus was crucified, buried, and raised from the dead; that He ascended to heaven and is today at the right hand of the Father as the Intercessor.
4. That all have sinned and come short of the glory of God, and that repentance is commanded by God for all and necessary for forgiveness of sins.
5. That justification, regeneration, and the new birth are wrought by faith in the blood of Jesus Christ.
6. In sanctification subsequent to the new birth, through faith in the blood of Christ; through the Word, and by the Holy Ghost.
7. Holiness to be God's standard of living for His people.
8. In the baptism of the Holy Ghost subsequent to a clean heart.
9. In speaking with other tongues as the Spirit gives utterance, and that is the initial evidence of the baptism of the Holy Ghost.
10. In water baptism by immersion, and all who repent should be baptized in the name of the Father, and of the Son, and of the Holy Ghost.
11. Divine healing is provided for all in the atonement.
12. In the Lord's Supper and washing of the saint's feet.
13. In the premillennial second coming of Jesus. First, to resurrect the righteous dead and to catch away the living saints to Him in the air. Second, to reign on the earth a thousand years.
14. In the bodily resurrection; eternal life for the righteous and eternal punishment for the wicked.

Deliverance Voice staff

EDITOR IN CHIEF	Apostle Arturo Skinner
EDITOR	Lelia Lockwood
YOUTH EDITOR	Dorothy Gilliard
ART DIRECTOR	Jasper Samuel
FREELANCE ARTIST	Jerome Boyd
PHOTOGRAPHERS	Gregory Griffith • Louis Anderson
PRESS OPERATORS	John Creamer • Charles Rhodes
COLUMNISTS	Corrine Austin • Ruth Harrison, Joann Stevens
VARITYPER	Vivian Bennett
PROOFREADER	Thelma Staples

Where there is faith
There is love
Where there is love
There is peace
Where there is peace
There is God
Where there is God
There is no need

We can make it through 1975 and the years that follow, (should Jesus tarry) as long as we keep the faith. Our faith is what supports and strengthens us in the love of God. We must KNOW God, and thus love him. (To know him is to love him) Faith tells us he does exist and that he is concerned about us. Faith tells us he is ready to grant a special healing touch, or to make plain his perfect will. At all times, faith is present even when we cannot "see" him. (On the left hand, where he doth work, but I cannot behold him: he hideth himself on the right hand, that I cannot see him: Job 23:9) — where there is faith there is love —

Love begets peace. (There is no fear in love; but perfect love casteth out fear: because fear hath torment. He that feareth is not made perfect in love. We love him, because he first loved us. — 1 John 4:18, 19) — To seek universal love or even brotherly love without the love of

Continued on page 24...

RECEIVE A MIRACLE—This very magazine was prayed over by Apostle Skinner, that God will work a supernatural miracle for you; even in your home and family. The DELIVERANCE VOICE comes to you from our National Headquarters and Temple where prayer and consecration are perpetual.

Building Faith For A Supernatural Deliverance.

Apostle Skinner Prays.

"But without faith it is impossible to please him: for he that cometh to God must believe that he is, and that he is a rewarder of them that diligently seek him". Hebrews 11:6 - God said, if he can find faith in the hearts of the people, I'll work miracles, I'll heal the sick, I'll deliver men and women, I'll raise the dead, but I want to find faith. Where God can find faith, He'll loose the bound and send the devil on his way. If He can find faith, He'll open that door that's been shut. But, we've got to have faith. Faith, and I'll go in the furnace with you and bring you out alright. Faith! "And Jesus said unto them, . . . If ye have faith as a grain of mustard seed, ye shall say unto this mountain, Remove hence to yonder place; and it shall remove; and NOTHING SHALL BE IMPOSSIBLE UNTO YOU." Matthew 17:20.

God said if He can find faith, you won't have to worry about this depression. God said, He'll bless you. He'll put food in the cupboard, (yes, He will). Money in your pocket, gas in your car! God said, if He can find faith, He'll save sinners. You might be in yonder's sanitorium. You might be behind prison walls; in your car, in the patio, in the field, wherever you are, lift your hands to the Lord, as a point of surrender. Lift your hands to heaven as to touch the hand of God. God said, He'll do what you want Him to do, that you might go out into the hedges and the highways, tell men and women that He's God and always will be God . . . that He neither slumbers nor sleeps. God, is the same yesterday, today and for ever.

Wherever you are lift your hands, whether you be a sinner or a backslider, or saint. To you that are not on the Lord's side. You that are still on the downward road to destruction. Take my advice: STOP, LOOK, AND LISTEN! God loves you. He loves you enough, that He sent Jesus into the world to die for you. "For God so loved the world, that he gave his only begotten Son, that whosoever believeth in him should not perish, but have everlasting life". St. John 3:16. All you've got to do is believe that He came, He died, He rose, and that His blood can save you. Wherever you are say "Lord have mercy upon me a sinner. Save me now for Christ's sake. I'm sorry for my sins, sorry enough that I want to quit. I want to turn from my sins and accept you as Lord of my life". The Bible says, ". . . and him that cometh to me I will in no wise cast out". St. John 6:37. If you're coming to Jesus, if you're coming right now. He's standing there to save you. He's standing ready to wash you in His Blood, and write your name in the Lamb's Book of Life. He'll give you the assurance that you have passed from death unto life.

To the dope addict, to the murderer, to the thief, the pimp, the pervert, to the street-walker, the SINNER . . . if you've asked Him to have mercy on you, if you meant it in your heart; you're SAVED right where you are.

To you that need a supernatural miracle, you that are physically sick. (The doctors have given you up), I've got news for you, you don't have to die. I know of a Saviour who is mighty

Continued on page 21...

Charismatic BACK TO GOD!
Madison Square Garden Crusades

WHAT'S ALL THE "TO DO" about? Why the urgent press of extensive crusading? Why the financial expense of Madison Square Garden? The answer vibrates deep within the heart of every believer: JESUS IS COMING. Yes, Jesus is soon to come. He will rapture the saints, and we will be glory bound. I don't know the exact hour of His return, but according to the signs of the times, (Matthew 24th chapter) it may be tomorrow, perhaps tonight, or even sooner.

The Madison Square Garden Crusades are drawing millions back to God. The charismatic outpourings experienced by those in attendance at the September Felt Forum Crusade, are but an invitation to get back to God. (Back to when we believed God can and will do anything but fail. Back to a fear and reverence for God and the Church. Back to a life of prayer and consecration. Back to sanctification and away from the "anything goes salvation". Back to the "ole time religion"; when we loved not only each other, but sinners too. Back to seeking God daily for direction to reach the lost. Back to living holy everyday and not just on Sunday).

The Felt Forum Crusade was the greatest evangelistic endeavor to date, conducted under the banner of Deliverance and the ministry of Evangelist Arturo Skinner. Sinners were saved. Cigarettes were thrown upon the altar, as the Holy Ghost sanctified and delivered. Alcoholics were "dried up" immediately, as God wrought supernatural miracles. Drug addicts, streetwalkers, the bound, the oppressed, the possessed, all found Christ, and He was glorified. Believers were encouraged, strengthened, healed and liberated.

Of the many that were healed and blessed, Miss Jacqueline Corbett of Newark, New Jersey testified of having received a very special blessing. She had been wearing glasses for four years, and obeyed Evangelist Skinner as he said, "take off your glasses and receive a miracle". Miss Corbett has not had to put her glasses back on, for God has supernaturally restored her eyesight.

As we continue to launch out in our outreach for the Mid-town New York Area be sure your name is on the DELIVERANCE VOICE mailing list, that you might be properly advised of our Crusade itinerary. Also, for your convenience, we have included the following forms that you might place the names of friends and acquaintances you wish to share the VOICE with.

ORDER FORM ON PAGE 9

All nationalities were represented for Evangelist Skinner's prayer!

Miss Corbett testifies, I know God works in the supernatural!

Ministers praised God for the supernatural signs, wonders, and miracles that happened nightly!

Massive Altar Call response. And this is why we came . . . to reach the lost!

A sinner finds Christ . . . thank God for saving him!

YOUTH COLUMN

DOROTHY GILLIARD
YOUTH EDITOR

PRAISE THE LORD my brothers and sisters in Christ! My heart is bubbling over with joy at the opportunity to write to you once more. It seems like ions since last I wrote and God has done much in my life over the months. I have a new inspiration; a new spiritual outlook on life; a new determination; and I'm rather anxious to share it ALL with you.

I have discovered even this year that to be young afforded me with great possibilities for success. Yes - within each one of us lies the potential to do great things for God. I am reminded of the story of an elderly schoolteacher who always reverently removed his hat before a company of young people, "not knowing", he said, "what future great man or woman might be among them."

Do you, young people, ever sit down in the quiet and think deeply and seriously about your life -- what it is, what wondrous powers are sleeping in your brain; in your heart; in your hands? Do you ever think what you may become, what you may do in this world?

A famous Christian writer once wrote, "Christian young life, given to Christ and touched by His hand and set apart in holy consecration to His alone for time and eternity - who can paint its glory?"

God is looking for people just like you and I! People who will ask Jesus what those valiant soldiers asked Him as he preached down by the Jordan River. They asked, "And what shall we do?"

The prophet Joel predicted that immediately prior to the coming of Christ, an army of men and women would be raised up to 'go out into all the world and preach the gospel to all nations.' They would be soldiers, equipped with the whole armor of God, and ready to do battle for the Lord. They would be filled with the Holy Spirit and endued with supernatural power. Right now, at this very moment God is recruiting young people to join His Army. Will you be one?

Joel described this 'Jesus Army' as a 'great and strong people' -- the likes of whom had not been seen before. A people that could 'run without getting weary;' that walked together with one collective goal in mind. They were to be an army led by God. Every soldier in this Army was to deliver the same message to the lost and dying souls of men, "Rend your heart, and turn unto the Lord your God; for He is gracious and merciful, slow to anger, and of great kindness . . ." This Jesus Army was to be comprised of soul-winners.

Can you be counted in this glorious number? Is Jesus Christ just in you or is He shining through you that others might see Him? Are you 'marking time' or are you ready for action? God is looking for youth who are willing to forsake all for the cause of Christ. People who feel the "urgency of the hour" and no longer want to sit about in idleness. Thousands of young people all over the world are turning on to Jesus and going out into God's vineyard to work. But thousands more just plain, "ain't doin' nothin'.

Jesus is coming really soon. I don't want Him to catch me with my work undone. No, I'm not looking for an extra starry crown when I get to heaven or a divine pat on the back. I just want to be able to say as Apostle Paul did, "For I am ready now to be offered, and the time of my departure is at hand. I have fought a good fight, I have finished my course, I have kept the faith."

Young people this is our opportunity to enlist in the service of God. Whether by means of sharing testimony, poetry, experiences, etc. Why not write and let us know what you're thinking. We're open for suggestions. LET US HEAR FROM YOU!

TO THOSE THAT NEED LEGAL HELP, CALL THE DELIVERANCE TEMPLE (201) 243-3777 or 243-3778

PANAMERICAN DELIVERANCE EVANGELISTIC CENTER TABERNACLE

The newly renovated premises located atop the Deliverance Tabernacle (785 DeKalb Avenue, Brooklyn, New York) will be presided over by Evangelist Prince Marshall, as it will house the PanAmerican Deliverance Evangelistic Center.

For the past ten years, Evangelist Marshall has blended his bilingual skills with the ministry of Apostle Skinner in that of interpreting for those of hispanic descent. The opening of the Pan American Deliverance Center is but another phase of Apostle's Skinner's ministry, and Evangelist Marshall feels himself but a representative of this same ministry to the hispanic people. This endeavor of faith, says Evangelist Marshall is yet another step in preparation for his ministry.

During each of our services, Evangelist Marshall welcomes our hispanic brethren in their native tongue and invites them to visit the PanAmerican Deliverance Center to continue their spiritual growth in God.

We salute the entire Marshall family, as they launch out to do the Master's will.

Evangelist Prince Marshall (center) interprets in Spanish, Apostle (left) Arturo Skinner's message preached in the Pan American Crusade held at the Brooklyn Deliverance Tabernacle.

START MAKING YOUR PLANS NOW...

DELIVERANCE CRUISE
FALL OF 1975
7 Day Caribbean Cruise
With Apostle Arturo Skinner!

SEPTEMBER 1976
First Holy Land Pilgrmage To Jerusalem
&
London, England & Rome

FOR MORE INFORMATION WRITE:
TRAVEL DEPARTMENT, DELIVERANCE TEMPLE HEADQUARTERS,
621 CLINTON AVE., NEWARK, N.J. 07108
Let us know you're planning to be with us.

NOW YOU CAN CALL THE
DELIVERANCE PRAYER TOWER

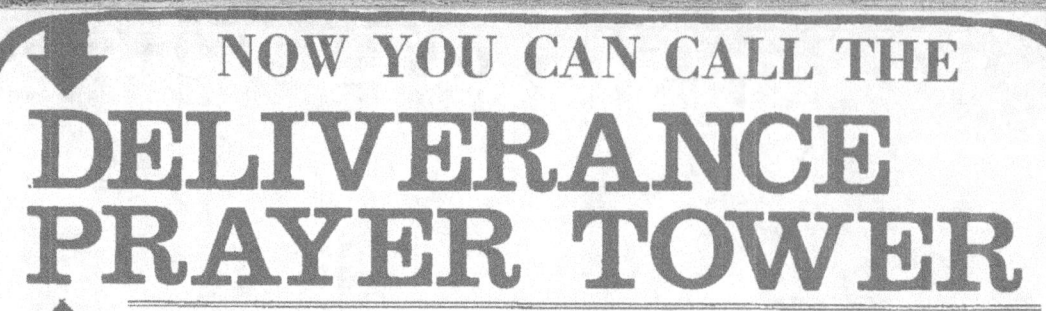

AT OUR
DELIVERANCE ADMINISTRATION BUILDING
NEWARK, NEW JERSEY

EVANGELIST KATIE HENRY
PRAYER TOWER DIRECTRESS

wires open
24 Hours Daily
7 days a week

✶ **(201)** ✶
243-3777 ✶ 243-3778

Be looking forward to...

DELIVERANCE AT MIDNIGHT
RADIO BROADCAST

Sponsored by the Deliverance Businessmen Fellowship.

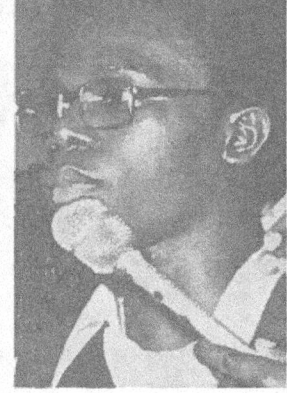

"Bound For Two Years By An Evil Condition"

My body itched day and night, and I could feel something crawling inside my stomach. My back was twisted out of shape, and I had to walk hunched over as though I was a crippled man. I couldn't even sit up in a chair. The doctor gave me pills, but the pills didn't help. I was in an anointing service that Reverend Skinner laid hands on me and commanded the devil to loose me in the Name of Jesus! God delivered me that night, and today I feel like a new man. When I look in the mirror, I can't believe my own eyes. I look different! Only a true man of God could have delivered me from the bonds of satan, and made me the free man I am today.

—Keith Wilson
Montclair, New Jersey

God Circulated Through My Bloodstream!

Because of a serious blood disorder, I was rushed to the hospital. Doctors said that my blood was too thick and that I had too much blood in my body. I was told of the danger of clot formation and of the possibility of death. My leg was swollen with excess blood, and I was in extreme pain... unable to walk. My husband got in touch with God's Apostle, and he prayed for me by telephone. In less than one hour God supernaturally thinned out my blood and the swelling went down in my leg. Today, I am back on my feet and praising God for my miracle.

—Lucy Cox
Somerset, New Jersey

GOD Answers Now!

My little boy fell and split his tongue partially in half. The gash was extremely deep and the left part of his tongue was hanging. His mouth was so swollen that he could not close it. My wife and I telephoned the Deliverance Prayer Tower leaving word for someone to get in touch with Reverend Skinner for us. The man of God returned the call that same day, and within ½ hour after he prayed, my son was COMPLETELY HEALED. There is no evidence that his tongue was ever hurt. We truly thank God for this dynamic deliverance.

—Nathaniel White
Bronx, New York

Charismatic Anointing Falls...

Deliverance Soul Winner's Bible Institute won't be the same!

Charisma draws hundreds to opening night of D.B.I.

"Not that we are sufficient of ourselves to think any thing as of ourselves; but our sufficiency is of God; Who also hath made us able ministers of the new testament; not of the letter, but of the spirit: for the letter killeth, but the spirit giveth life." 2 Corinthians 3:5,6.

Apostle Skinner has received word from God concerning the administrative and educational program of the Deliverance Bible Institute. In effect, God has said there are thousands of Bible schools where students may attend to receive credits and coveted degrees. The Deliverance Bible Institute will of course, continue to offer its students the best possible study material and techniques. However, God has ordained that the entire student body and faculty as well, concentrate on seeking the *charismatic* anointing of the Holy Ghost.

It is going to take the *charismatic* anointing of the Holy Ghost to win the lost for Christ. Zechariah 4:6 reminds us that it is "not by might, nor by power, but by my spirit, saith the LORD of hosts."

It will take the *charismatic* anointing to effectively "preach good tidings to the meek: ... to bind up the brokenhearted, to proclaim liberty to the captives, and the opening of the prison to them that are bound; To proclaim the acceptable year of the LORD, and the day of vengeance of our God; to comfort all that mourn; To appoint unto them that mourn in Zion, to give unto them beauty for ashes, the oil of joy for mourning, the garment of praise for the spirit of heaviness; that they might be called trees of righteousness, the planting of the LORD, that he might be glorified. c.f. Isaiah 61:1-3.

Hence, the Deliverance Bible Institute and its entire outreach will be Holy Ghost oriented; inspired; presented, and delivered. If you want your ministry to be propelled by the unction of the Holy Ghost, attend D.B.I. Don't expect its courses to be like any you have witnessed, but expect to see God in action. ■

PRESIDENT & FOUNDER
Apostle Arturo Skinner

PRINCIPAL
Evang. Audrey Thoroughgood

FACULTY
Evang. Elaine Thomas
Evang. Edna Smith
Evang. Marlene Bannister
Evang. Lucille Garrett
Evang. Marguerite Covington
Evang. William McNair
Evang. John Blaine

BUILDING FAITH...

DELIVERANCE PUBLISHING HOUSE

PRESS - TIM DAVIS (L) AND JOHN CREAMER (R) INSPECTS PRESS PROOF

PLATE MAKING - CHARLES RHODES ADJUSTS "FLATS" FOR MAKING OF PLATES

STRIPPING — SESREA (L) AND TIM (R) OPAQUE AND STRIP NEGATIVES

CUTTING - CHARLES PREPARES PRINTED SHEETS OF PAPER FOR CUTTER

FOLDING - SESREA MILLER OPERATES FOLDING MACHINE WHICH FOLDS PRINTED LITERATURE.

The ministry of printed page is as exciting as it is vast. Headed by John Creamer, the publishing staff aspires to keep the world abreast of the *charismatic* enterprises of Deliverance Evangelism Internationally. So diverse are the many facets of Apostle Skinner's ministry, that only God could so organize and bring to pass all that we see unfolding before our eyes. The ultimate is the saving of souls. 100,000,000 souls for Christ is our goal. The publishing aspect is possibly the closest department to the man of God for it carries him into homes, villages, and even huts of those who may never have the opportunity to visit the Temple or attend a Crusade.

Behind the scenes, it is business unusual. Sheet music, books, advertisements, DELIVERANCE VOICE, stationery, plate making, photography, press, hardly encompass all efforts being spent to support and present the ministry.

The Publishing House is located within the Deliverance Temple Headquarters, 621 Clinton Avenue, Newark, New Jersey.

JANUARY/FEBRUARY, 1975

And he said unto them, go ye into all the world, and preach the gospel to every creature. St. Mark 16:15

Be looking & praying for the **DELIVERANCE EVANGELISTIC REVIVAL CENTER TABERNACLES** that will be opening in your area.

California
- LOS ANGELES
- OAKLAND
- SAN DIEGO
- SAN FRANCISCO

Connecticut
- BRIDGEPORT
- HARTFORD
- STANFORD

Delaware
- WILMINGTON

Florida
- MIAMI
- ORLANDO

Georgia
- ATLANTA
- AUGUSTA
- LYONS
- MACON

Illinois
- CHICAGO
- ROBBINS

Indiana
- GARY

Louisiana
- BATON ROUGE
- NEW ORLEANS

Maryland
- BALTIMORE

Massachusetts
- BOSTON
- SPRINGFIELD

Michigan
- DETROIT
- E. DETROIT

Mississippi
- JACKSON

New Jersey
- ATLANTIC CITY
- CAMDEN
- ENGLEWOOD
- HOBOKEN
- JERSEY CITY
- LAKEWOOD
- LINDEN
- LONG BRANCH
- NEWARK
- RED BANK
- ROSELLE
- SOMERSET
- SUMMIT
- TRENTON

New York
- ALBANY
- BRONX
- BROOKLYN
- BUFFALO
- E. HARLEM
- FAR ROCKAWAY
- FREEPORT (Queens)
- LONG ISLAND CITY
- NEW YORK CITY (MID-TOWN)
- PANAMERICAN CENTER (B'klyn)
- RED HOOK (B'klyn)
- RIVERHEAD
- SCHENECTADY
- STATEN ISLAND
- TROY

North Carolina
- ASHBORO
- ENGELHARD
- KENANSVILLE
- OXFORD
- SCOTLAND NECK
- SCRANTON
- WARSAW
- WASHINGTON

South Carolina
- BENNETSVILLE
- ESTILL
- HOPKINS
- MONKS CORNER

Ohio
- AKRON
- CLEVELAND
- COLUMBUS
- TOLEDO
- YOUNGSTOWN

Pennsylvania
- ALIQUIPPA
- BETHLEHEM
- CHESTER
- COATESVILLE
- HARRISBURG
- LANCASTER
- PHILADELPHIA
- PITTSBURGH
- READING

Texas
- HOUSTON

Virginia
- CHARLOTTESVILLE
- KENBRIDGE
- LOVINGSTON
- LYNCHBURG
- NORFOLK
- RICHMOND
- ROANOKE

West Virginia
- BERKELEY
- WIERTON

Washington
- SEATTLE

Washington, D.C.

OVERSEAS CENTERS
- AFRICA
- ETHIOPIA
- LOGOS, NIGERIA
- KENYA
- S. AFRICA
- BRAZIL
- CANADA
- COSTA RICA
- ENGLAND
- GHANA, W.A.
- HAITI
- HAWAII
- KOREA
- MEXICO
- PUERTO RICO
- WEST INDIES
  - BARBADOS
  - ST. THOMAS
  - JAMAICA
- SAN DOMINGO

Deliverance Forerunner Team

Evangelist
Clyde Moore

Evangelist
Marguerite Covington

Evangelist
Stephen Jackson

The above forerunners are unanimous in their zeal to reach the lost. The good samaritan ministry is unique in itself, as many would rather hurriedly pass by than to take the time to tell a sinner, (drunkard, beggar, street-walker or pimp) that Jesus cares for them. That Jesus died for their sins, just as He died for yours and mine. It is impossible to document the tedious hours put into these evangelists' efforts.

The forerunners prepare the way for Apostle Skinner's crusades. They spend time, (on a one to one basis) to exhibit love and concern for their fellow man.

We especially request your prayers for the Deliverance forerunners and their co–workers as they labor for the souls of men.

...whatever the need.

THE SUPERNATURAL DELIVERANCE PRAYER TOWER IS READY TO UNITE WITH YOU IN PRAYER FOR YOUR NEEDS, WHATEVER THE NATURE, AT ANY HOUR DAY AND NIGHT!

CALL:
Area Code (201)
243-3777 or
243-3778

"AND GOD WROUGHT Supernatural Miracles

by the hands of Paul; so that from his body were brought unto the sick handkerchiefs or aprons and the diseases departed from them, and the evil spirits went out of them..." —Acts 19:11, 12

As an Apostle of Jesus Christ, I am always receiving calls to go into the hospitals and homes to pray for the sick and other cases. It would be wonderful if I could go everywhere, into every home, and hospital and personally lay my hands upon each one in prayer, I CANNOT.

Therefore, I am sending and giving out SUPERNATURAL PRAYER CLOTHS. And the reports are coming in from far and near of many being supernaturally blessed and helped; many kinds of sicknesses are being healed. The lame are made to walk, and testimonies are being received of death bed cases raised up. SUPERNATURAL PRAYER CLOTHS are used by faith in THE NAME OF JESUS.

Operations are being cancelled. Many are blessed financially! Peace is being brought into troubled homes! But, it doesn't stop there, YOU can be blessed if you use this SUPERNATURAL PRAYER CLOTH in faith.*

*When you are helped through this SUPERNATURAL PRAYER CLOTH give God the praise, and let me know about it.

TO RECEIVE YOUR FREE
SUPERNATURAL PRAYER CLOTH

MAIL TO:
Apostle Arturo Skinner
785 DeKalb Avenue
Brooklyn, New York 11221

NAME_____
ADDRESS_____
CITY_____ STATE_____ ZIP_____
MY PRAYER REQUEST IS: _____
_____
_____

Call the Executive Office for information regarding:

Deliverance Enterprises

(201) 243-1300 (212) 782-6300

Business Organization & Management (Consultant)	Dressmaking	Paintings (Original)
Accountant (CPA) (Auditing, Tax returns, etc.)	Economist	Photography
Antiques & Thrift Shop	Employment Agency	Plastering Services
Carpentry	Floor Waxing	Plumbing
Carpet Cleaning	Freelance Typing	Public Relations
Cassette Services	Furs	Promotion (Sales)
Catering (Pvt. Affairs, Dinners, Banquets, etc.)	Giles Furniture House	Radio & Television Repair
Commercial Art (Signs, etc.)	Giles Moving Company	Real Estate
Contractors	Interior Decorators	Records
Deliverance Publishing House	Irons Works	Recording Company
Deliverance School Of Fashion	Masonry	Restaurants
Deliverance Travel Agency	Marketing, Management, Merchandising	Roofing
	Millinary, Modeling	Wedding Consultant (Counselling, Arrangements, Catering, etc.)
	Music Shop	
	Painting Services (Household)	

1975 Looking Forward To 100 Businesses Under One Roof.

Directory Of Deliverance
Pastors & Their Church Areas

DELIVERANCE EVANGELISTIC CENTER
785 DEKALB AVENUE
BROOKLYN, NEW YORK

REV. LILLIE AMBERS
MONTCLAIR, NEW JERSEY

REV. LANDORE A. BELL
SAN NICOLAS, ARUBA N. A.

REV. ELOIS BELLAMY
NEW BRUNSWICK, NEW JERSEY

REV. BENJAMIN BETHEA
LANCASTER, PENNSYLVANIA

REV. NAN BETTERSON
BEACON, NEW YORK

REV. RAY BLAKE
MT. VERNON, NEW YORK
STANFORD, CONNECTICUT

REV. JOHN BLAINE
LANCASTER, PENNSYLVANIA

REV. O'DELL BRADLEY
PRINCETON, NEW JERSEY

REV. RONALD BROWN
ORANGEBURG, SOUTH CAROLINA
SAVANNAH, GEORGIA

REV. HERMAN CARTER
FREEPORT, LONG ISLAND N.Y.

REV. HOWARD CONNELLY
STATEN ISLAND, NEW YORK

REV. SEVILLA COOK
MIAMI, FLORIDA
HOLLYWOOD, FLORIDA

EVANG. CARL DALLAS
WASHINGTON, D.C.

REV. BIRDIE DAVIS
NEWARK, NEW JERSEY

REV. EUGENE STACKHOUSE
JERSEY CITY, NEW JERSEY

REV. ROWLEY C. DUKE
TRINIDAD, W.I.

REV. FINNEY T. ISRAEL
DISTRICT S. INDIA

REV. RUBY FLUKER
MOBILE, ALABAMA

REV. KENNETH FLYTH
NORFOLK, VIRGINIA

REV. RICHARD GLOVER
COLUMBIA, SOUTH CAROLINA

EVANG. LOIS GOODEN
LEXINGTON, NORTH CAROLINA

REV. & EVANG. AUGUSTUS GOODSON
HOPKINS, SOUTH CAROLINA

REV. CLYDE GRAY
MATTSPAN, MASSACHUSETTS

REV. ROBERT GREENE
MELBOURNE, FLORIDA

REV. PETER HALLENBACK
ALIQUIPPA, PENNSYLVANIA

REV. LEON HATTEN
NEWARK, NEW JERSEY
RIVERHEAD, LONG ISLAND, N.Y.
WYANDANCH, LONG ISLAND, N.Y.

REV. JAMES HILTON
FAYETTEVILLE, NORTH CAROLINA

REV. JOHN HORNE
TRENTON, NEW JERSEY

EVANG. NATHAN JACKSON
ELIZABETH, NEW JERSEY

REV. MATTHEW JOHNSON
HOLLIS, LONG ISLAND, N.Y.
HEMPSTEAD, LONG ISLAND

REV. JACKIE JORDAN
CHICAGO, ILLINOIS

MILDRED KERRY
DETROIT, MICHIGAN

REV. WILLIE C. LEWIS
DURHAM, NORTH CAROLINA

REV. ERSKINE MARS
BROOKLYN, NEW YORK

REV. PRINCE MARSHALL
BROOKLYN, NEW YORK

EVANG. WILLIAM McLAIN
CHARLOTTE, NORTH CAROLINA

EVANG. EDWARD McNAIR
WINSTON SALEM, NORTH CAROLINA

REV. LORRAINE MORRISON
NEWPORT NEWS, VIRGINIA

REV. FLORENCE MORRISON
ORANGE, NEW JERSEY

EVANG. RALPH NICHOLS
NEWARK, NEW JERSEY

EVANG. V. PERRY
KOREA

REV. JEWEL NICKELS
NEWARK, NEW JERSEY

EVANG. LOUISE NICKENS
APOPKA, FLORIDA

REV. JOHN OWENS
FLORENCE, SOUTH CAROLINA

REV. MARY PARKER
ROCKY MOUNT, NORTH CAROLINA

REV. CHRISTINA PHILLIPS
BALTIMORE, MARYLAND

REV. HINJON POOSER
HOLLY HILL, SOUTH CAROLINA

EVANG. ELONORA PRATT
PHILADELPHIA, PENNSYLVANIA

REV. SALMON PRESENT
SOUTH AFRICA

REV. ELIZABETH RAY
JAMAICA, LONG ISLAND

REV. WALTER SCOTT
PATERSON, NEW JERSEY

REV. THEOLDO SHEAFE
BROOKLYN, NEW YORK

REV. JAMES SHECKLEFORD SR.
PHILADELPHIA, PENNSYLVANIA

REV. FLOYD SHERROD
BUFFALO, NEW YORK

REV. COLUMBUS SHIELDS
SUMERSET, NEW JERSEY

EVANG. RUBY SHELTON
VIRGINIA

REV. DORSEY SHOULTZ
CAMDEN, NEW JERSEY

EVANG. ANTHEA SIMMONS
TRINIDAD, W.I.

APOSTLE ARTURO SKINNER
BROOKLYN, NEW YORK

EVANG. EDNA SMITH
SALEM, NEW JERSEY

REV. HERBERT SNEED
ASBURY PARK, NEW JERSEY

REV. LONNIE TALLEY
NEW HAVEN, CONNECTICUT

REV. MRS. RICHARD TAYLOR
POUGHKEEPSIE, NEW YORK
NEWBURGH, NEW YORK

REV. HARRY THOMPSON
STATEN ISLAND, NEW YORK

REV. LOUISE TILLERY
CLINTON, NORTH CAROLINA

EVANG. PAULINE TROTTER
JACKSON, MISSISSIPPI

EVANG. IRSOME TUKES
BROOKLYN, NEW YORK

REV. PHILLIP TURNER
PLAINFIELD, NEW JERSEY

EVANG. MAMIE RUTH WESTON
ENGLEHARD, NORTH CAROLINA

EVANG. JAMES WHITE
ELIZABETH, NEW JERSEY

REV. NATHANIEL WHITE
BRONX, NEW YORK

REV. WILLIE J. WILLIAMS
NEW YORK, NEW YORK

REV. W.T. WILLIAMS
NEW YORK, NEW YORK

EVANG. THOMAS WRIGHT
PERTH AMBOY, NEW JERSEY

EVANG. HENRY WRIGHT
VALDOSTA, GEORGIA

EVANG. WALTER SIMMONS
LONG ISLAND, NEW YORK

FOR FURTHER INFORMATION CALL: (212) 782-6300 or (201) 243-1300

Miracles Happen At The Deliverance Prayer Tower!

The Prayer Tower of the Deliverance Evangelistic Center stands as a symbol of warmth, light, and hope to people in the states and across the world.

When you need someone to pray—to care for your hurts and needs... Remember THE DELIVERANCE PRAYER TOWER is open 24 hours a day, every day of the year (...even in the midnight hours...) because God has raised up this ministry to care and to pray for you...and to help you get to God, the SOURCE of all healing and Deliverance!

Anytime a loved one, friend or you have a need, just call. We are here to minister to you!

Someone

Someone walks beside me,
Someone holds my hand,
Someone leads and guides me
   over this troubled land.
Though His face I cannot see,
   His touch I can feel,
And I know that it's Jesus, who's
   walking beside me, as I walk
   up the hill.

Someone lifts my heavy burdens,
Someone wipes away my tears,
Someone never leaves me alone and
   never lets me fear.
Though His face I cannot see,
   His voice I can hear,
And I know that it's Jesus, who keeps
   me in His ever loving care.

Someone knows my every weakness,
Someone hears my call,
Someone walks with me through the
   valleys and never lets me fall.
Though His face I cannot see,
   He's standing close by,
And I know that it's Jesus, who hears
   my every cry.

Someone calms the angry storm,
Someone whispers be still my heart,
Someone lets me know that I'm His
   and from Him can never part.
Though His face I cannot see, I
   know He's on my side,
And I know that it's Jesus, who turns
   the raging tide.

Charismatic BACK TO GOD!
Madison Square Garden Crusades

WHAT'S ALL THE "TO DO" about? Why the urgent press of extensive crusading? Why the financial expense of Madison Square Garden? The answer vibrates deep within the heart of every believer: JESUS IS COMING. Yes, Jesus is soon to come. He will rapture the saints, and we will be glory bound. I don't know the exact hour of His return, but according to the signs of the times, (Matthew 24th chapter) it may be tomorrow, perhaps tonight, or even sooner.

The Madison Square Garden Crusades are drawing millions back to God. The charismatic outpourings experienced by those in attendance at the September Felt Forum Crusade, are but an invitation to get back to God. (Back to when we believed God can and will do anything but fail. Back to a fear and reverence for God and the Church. Back to a life of prayer and consecration. Back to sanctification and away from the "anything goes salvation". Back to the "ole time religion"; when we loved not only each other, but sinners too. Back to seeking God daily for direction to reach the lost. Back to living holy everyday and not just on Sunday).

The Felt Forum Crusade was the greatest evangelistic endeavor to date, conducted under the banner of Deliverance and the ministry of Evangelist Arturo Skinner. Sinners were saved. Cigarettes were thrown upon the altar, as the Holy Ghost sanctified and delivered. Alcoholics were "dried up" immediately, as God wrought supernatural miracles. Drug addicts, streetwalkers, the bound, the oppressed, the possessed, all found Christ, and He was glorified. Believers were encouraged, strengthened, healed and liberated.

Of the many that were healed and blessed, Miss Jacqueline Corbett of Newark, New Jersey testified of having received a very special blessing. She had been wearing glasses for four years, and obeyed Evangelist Skinner as he said, "take off your glasses and receive a miracle". Miss Corbett has not had to put her glasses back on, for God has supernaturally restored her eyesight.

As we continue to launch out in our outreach for the Mid-town New York Area be sure your name is on the DELIVERANCE VOICE mailing list, that you might be properly advised of our Crusade itinerary. Also, for your convenience, we have included the following forms that you might place the names of friends and acquaintances you wish to share the VOICE with.

ORDER FORM ON PAGE 9

All nationalities were represented for Evangelist Skinner's prayer!

Miss Corbett testifies, I know God works in the supernatural!

Ministers praised God for the supernatural signs, wonders, and miracles that happened nightly!

Massive Altar Call response. And this is why we came... to reach the lost! A sinner finds Christ... thank God for saving him!

Charismatic testimonies tell the story of the supernatural anointing in the ministry of Evangelist Arturo Skinner. The oppression of sin, sickness and disease must take flight as the man of God takes authority against all that is contrary to God's will. **"Beloved, I wish above all things that thou mayest prosper and be in health, even as thy soul prospereth."** —3 John 2

The following testimonies are given to inspire, encourage and strengthen you concerning the Deliverances of God!

Anniversary Testimony Of Healing One Year Ago: BONE CANCER

I just had to come back and celebrate my anniversary with Reverend Skinner and the saints of Deliverance. One year ago, I was at the end of my rope. My prognosis was grave, or doctors had given me six weeks to live. I had bone cancer. So eaten away with cancer was I, that my very bones had severed because of it. My wife and I heard about Reverend Skinner, and traveled from Virginia to the Brooklyn Tabernacle. It was there God met me, Reverend Skinner prayed, and God did the rest. I returned to the hospital for x-rays. The tests I was given, all proved negative. The same doctors gave me a clean bill of health. Since then, I have gained thirty-eight pounds. I feel brand new. The doctors are so amazed at this supernatural happening, that they want Reverend Skinner to come to Petersburg, and pray for the patients in the hospital.

—James Butler
Petersburg, Virginia

Youngest Ex-Drug Addict In Deliverance!

My 8-month-old nephew is now an ex-dope addict. He was born addicted to drugs because his mother was hooked on hard Skinner for prayer. When the man of God prayed, the child was completely delivered. He is free from the perils of drug addiction.

Prayer Instantly... Uproots Growth!

I had a growth on my neck for over 40 years. It was such a nuisance to me and in recent years began to pain and give discomfort. When I attended the Tuesday night anointing service I asked Reverend Skinner to especially pray for me. When he laid hands on the growth,

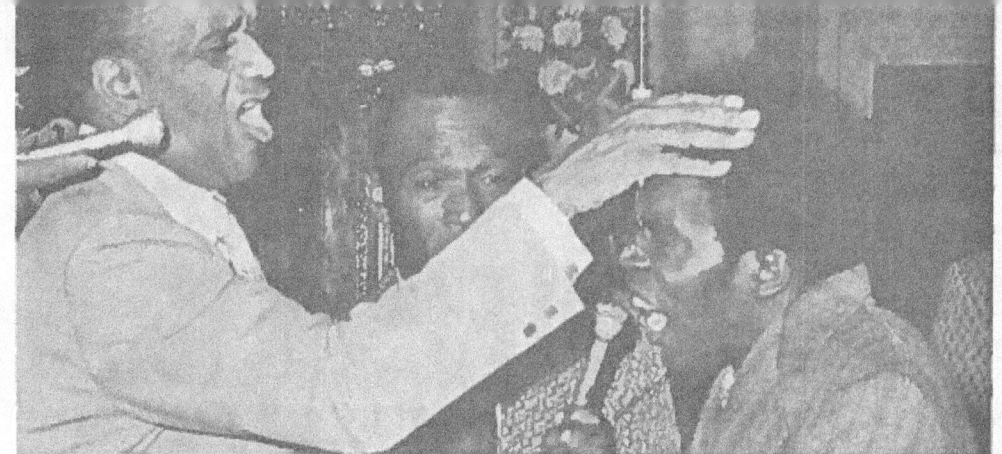 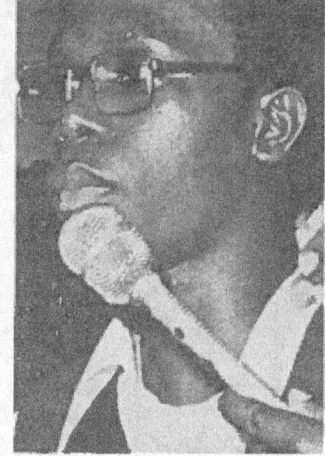

"Bound For Two Years By An Evil Condition"

My body itched day and night, and I could feel something crawling inside my stomach. My back was twisted out of shape, and I had to walk hunched over as though I was a crippled man. I couldn't even sit up in a chair. The doctor gave me pills, but the pills didn't help. It was in an anointing service that Reverend Skinner laid hands on me and commanded the devil to loose me in the Name of Jesus! God delivered me that night, and today I feel like a new man. When I look in the mirror, I can't believe my own eyes. I look different! Only a true man of God could have delivered me from the bonds of satan, and made me the free man I am today.

—Keith Wilson
Montclair, New Jersey

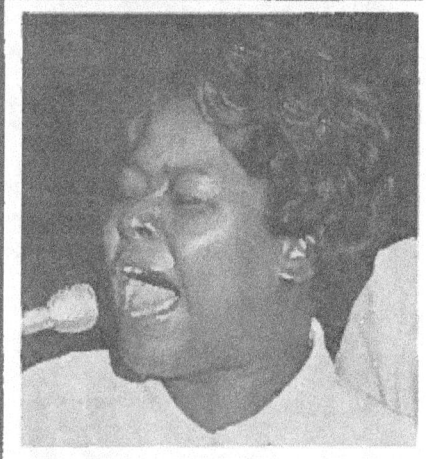

God Circulated Through My Bloodstream!

Because of a serious blood disorder, I was rushed to the hospital. Doctors said that my blood was too thick and that I had too much blood in my body. I was told of the danger of clot formation and of the possibility of death. My leg was swollen with excess blood, and I was in extreme pain... unable to walk. My husband got in touch with God's Apostle, and he prayed for me by telephone. In less than one hour God supernaturally thinned out my blood and the swelling went down in my leg.

GOD Answers Now!

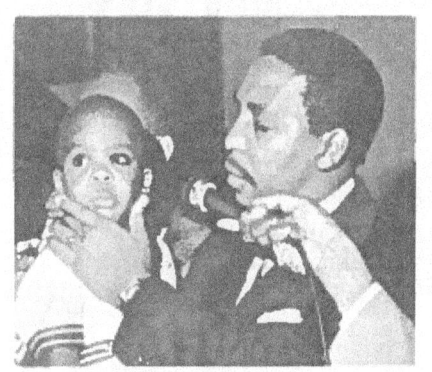

My little boy fell and split his tongue partially in half. The gash was extremely deep and the left part of his tongue was hanging. His mouth was so swollen that he could not close it. My wife and I telephoned the Deliverance Prayer Tower leaving word for someone to same day, and within ½ hour after he prayed, my son was COMPLETELY HEALED. There is no evidence that his tongue was ever hurt. We truly thank God for this

10,000 Volunteers

A volunteer is one who responds to a need with an enthusiasm above and beyond the call of duty. A volunteer team is composed of those dedicated to perform an extraordinary task. It is thus by no accident, the Deliverance Volunteer Members are doing such an excellent job in financial and prayerful support of the ministry. Headed by Mother Evelyn Tosson (Newark, New Jersey Area), and Evangelists Eugene Bell, and Steven Hawkins (Brooklyn, New York Area) monthly support may be counted on.

Deliverance Volunteers workers are composed of members of the church as well as well-wishers who are concerned about the souls of men. Crusading expenses are especially the burden of this organism, for it was through this ministry many of them were saved. Won't you become a member of the Volunteers? They extend to you this invitation to help reach the lost for Christ. The following testimony is that of a young man who excitedly proclaims the blessings he received in standing by Evangelist Skinner's ministry.

I'm Beautifully Blessed

"I've been a member of the Volunteers of Deliverance for 2 years. Since standing at the man of God's side financially, I am beautifully blessed. I was hired as the Custodian of the Temple. I have a beautiful salary, I can't complain about anything. I have six children, and they are Jr. Volunteers. My family is healthy and we know it is because we are helping to reach the masses for Christ."

Milton Baldwin, Bloomfield, N.J.

VOLUNTEER!
Become A Deliverance Volunteer!

GOD NEEDS YOU

Help Further The Gospel Of Jesus Christ!

SEND A MONTHLY CONTRIBUTION TO EVANGELIST ARTURO SKINNER

MY MONTHLY PLEDGE: $ _____
$5☐ $10☐ $15☐ $20☐ $25☐ $100☐ $500☐ $1000☐

Name _____
Address _____
City _____ State _____ Zip _____

MAIL TO: Evangelist Arturo Skinner,
621 Clinton Avenue, Newark, New Jersey 07180

Evangelist Of The Month

We are happy to salute Evangelist James E. White and Party, as they have been laboring in the Elizabeth, New Jersey Area in street meetings, and conducting Deliverance Rallies. Accounts have been coming in of back sliders returning to the fold; of sinners being saved and various healings.

Evangelist White is amazed that until 1963, he had a speech impediment, and it was very difficult for him to talk. At that time he came to Pastor Skinner simply because he was in need of healing. God not only healed him, but called James to the ministry and he hasn't stopped telling the Good News.

AWAITING THE Charismatic Baptism

"And I will pray the Father, and he shall give you another Comforter, that he may abide with you for ever..." St. John 14:16.

Every aspect of this last day Back to God revival is dependant upon the *charismatic* outpouring as foretold in Joel 2:28 "And it shall come to pass afterward, that I will pour out my spirit upon all flesh; and your sons and your daughters shall prophesy, your old men shall dream dreams, your young men shall see visions; And also upon the servants and upon the handmaids in those days will I pour out my spirit." People are coming from near and far, to the great tarry services being conducted in the Temple in Newark on Friday nights, and the Tabernacle in Brooklyn on Saturdays afternoons following the 2:30 services. They come seeking God in faith for the baptism of the Holy Ghost; seeking depths in the Holy Ghost, and seeking the perfect will of God.

Let's face it. If we are to get back to God, if we are to receive that *charismatic* anointing, we must first adhere to the Word of God in 2 Chronicles 7:14 "If my people, which are called by my name, shall humble themselves, and pray, and seek my face, and turn from their wicked ways; then will I hear from heaven, and will forgive their sin, and will heal their land." Not until we are charged up with the Holy Ghost, are we equipped to carry out whatever function (large or small) God has designated we perform in and/or out of church, and ultimately the reaching of souls.

Doors open for prayer every Monday, Tuesday, and Friday 12 noon at the Deliverance Temple - 621 Clinton Avenue, Newark, New Jersey and following every 2:30 P.M. service on Saturday at the Deliverance Tabernacle, 785 DeKalb Avenue, Brooklyn, New Jersey. ■

...whatever the need.

THE SUPERNATURAL DELIVERANCE PRAYER TOWER IS READY TO UNITE WITH YOU IN PRAYER FOR YOUR NEEDS, WHATEVER THE NATURE, AT ANY HOUR DAY AND NIGHT!

CALL:
Area Code (201)
243-3777 or
243-3778

IS YOUR WILL GOD'S WILL?

God's will for you is an expression of His love for you. You in turn may express your love for God and your fellow man by taking the necessary steps to prepare a will with the Charismatic Ministry of Deliverance in mind. (We suggest you seek the assistance of a qualified attorney). Your will CAN and WILL serve as a testimony of your personal helping ministry in the outreach for souls ripe and ready for harvest.

CLIP OUT AND SEND COUPON
FOR FURTHER INFORMATION!
(free of charge)
MAIL TO: LEGAL DEPARTMENT
NATIONAL HEADQUARTERS DELIVERANCE TEMPLE
621 CLINTON AVENUE/NEWARK, NEW JERSEY 07108

NAME_____
ADDRESS_____
CITY_____ STATE_____ ZIP_____

The Deliverance Radio Outreach Ministry
A NEW BEGINNING

by JIMMIE GILLIARD

The year nineteen-hundred-and-fifty-six (1956) was a very good year, for in that year the Deliverance Radio Outreach Ministry was born in the heart and soul of God's Apostle Rev. Arturo Skinner. Eighteen years ago the Hour of Deliverance was heard over a single station but the program has "snowballed" into a major salvation, deliverance, and blessing endeavour.

Today, the Hour of Deliverance radio broadcast can be heard by over 552 million people in 49 states, the West Indies, Europe, Africa, Canada, and South America. Why is our ministry so expansive? Because God has raised up Rev. Skinner to 'blanket the whole earth with the message of Deliverance'. The black, white, red, yellow; the rich, poor; the intellectual and the illiterate must know who Jesus is. Everybody outside of the "arch of safety" ought to know who He is. Paul said, "Unto me, who am less than the least of all, saints, is this grace given, that I should preach among the Gentiles, the unsearchable riches of Christ; and to make all men see what is the fellowship of the mystery, which from the beginning of the world hath been hid in God, who created all things by Jesus Christ." These could very easily be the words of Rev. Skinner because he has no other desire than the desire to reach the lost for Christ (at any cost.)

I celebrate the Deliverance Radio Outreach ministry because I remember what it was, I see how glorious it is now, and I rejoice over the new things that God is going to do for us. I'm so glad that God has saved me and brought me into the place where I can help this great man of God reach the lost souls through the media of radio.

The world needs Christ and I can find no more effective way of presenting Christ to the world than by radio. Perhaps one man can't save the whole world but there's nothing wrong with having the desire to do so. I've never met a man so determined to do God's Will; so burdened for the sinners; so zealous; so inspired; as God's Apostle. My heart is fixed and my mind is made up to go forth at his side and help him blanket the earth with the message of Deliverance.

Yes, we've come a long way with God's help and in the years to come we shall endeavour to do even greater works for the Lord through radio. Even right now my radio staff and I are feverishly working and praying to produce 'Deliverance at Midnight', our very own radio show. Pray for us. ■

DELIVERANCE CARES!

APOSTLE ARTURO SKINNER (RIGHT) AND REV. MILTON HICKS (LEFT) INSPECTS THE FOOD AND CLOTHING GOING TO THE POOR.

1 TON OF FOOD AND CLOTHING SENT TO...
HONDURAS, HAITI, WEST AFRICA, INDIA & UNITED STATES

Clothing was rushed to Honduras in emergency supply because of the flood victims of hurricane fifi in September. The Charismatic Deliverance Bible School rallied in prayerful support, and within 3 class nights brought in barrels of food stuffs, etc. The response was so great that we were able also, to send "Deliverance Care packages" to Haiti, West Africa, India and to the needy right here in the United States.

The Supernatural Hour Of Deliverance!
HEARD WEEKLY WITH EVANGELIST ARTURO SKINNER

ALABAMA
Station - WGOK - 900 KC
Sunday 10:30 A.M.

ARKANSAS
Little Rock - KAAY - 1090 KC
Sunday 10:30 P.M.

CALIFORNIA
San Francisco - KFAX - 1100 KC
Saturday 11:30 A.M.

Los Angeles - KDAY - 1580 HKZ
Sunday 9:00 A.M.

CANADA
Station - KAAY - 1090 KC
Sunday 10:30 P.M.

COLORADO
Denver - KQXI - 1550 KC
Saturday 1:30 P.M.
Sunday 4:30 P.M.

CONNECTICUT
Station - WRYT - 950 KC
Sunday 3:00 P.M.

DELAWARE
Station - WEBB - 1360 KC
Sunday 10:30 A.M.

FLORIDA
Miami - WRHC - 1550 KC
Sunday 9:30 A.M.

Orlando - WOKB - 1600 KC
Sunday 7:30 A.M.

Jacksonville - WERD - 1430 KC
Sunday 10:30 A.M.

GEORGIA
Augusta - WRDW - 1480 KC
Sunday 10:30 A.M.

Dublin - WXLI - 1230 KC
Sunday 6:30 P.M.

Macon - WIBB - 1280 KHZ
Sunday 8:30 A.M.

Savannah - WEAS - FM - 93.1
Sunday 10:30 A.M.

ILLINOIS
Chicago - WBEE - 1570 KC
Sunday 9:30 A.M.

Robbins - WBEE - 1570 KC
Sunday 9:30 A.M.

INDIANA
Gary - WBEE - 1570 KC
Sunday 9:30 A.M.

KENTUCKY
Station - WDIA - 1270 KC
Sunday 12:00 P.M.

LOUISIANA
Station - WDIA - 1270 KC
Sunday 12:00 P.M.

Station - KAAY - 1090 KC
Sunday 10:30 P.M.

MAINE
Station - WRYT - 950 KC
Sunday 3:00 P.M.

MARYLAND
Baltimore - WEBB - 1360 KC
Sunday 10:30 A.M.

MASSACHUSETTS
Boston - WRYT - 950 KC
Sunday 3:00 P.M.

MICHIGAN
Detroit - WCHB - 1440 KHZ
Sunday 11:30 P.M.

MINNESOTA
Station - KAAY - 1090 KC
Sunday 10:30 P.M.

Minneapolis - KUXL - 1570 KC
Sunday 9:30 A.M.

MISSISSIPPI
Station - WDIA - 1270 KC
Sunday 12:00 P.M.

Station - KAAY - 1090 KC
Sunday 10:30 P.M.

MISSOURI
Station - KAAY - 1090 KC
Sunday 10:30 P.M.

St. Louis - KXEN - 1010 KC
Sunday 9:30 A.M.

NEW HAMPSHIRE
Station - WRYT - 950 KC
Sunday 3:00 P.M.

NEW JERSEY
Station - WADO - 1280 KC
Sunday 10:00 P.M.

NEW YORK
New York City - WADO - 1280KC
Sunday 10:00 P.M.

NORTH CAROLINA
Greenville - WNCT - 1070 KC
Sunday 9:30 A.M.

OHIO
Akron - WCUE - FM - 96.5 MEG.
Sunday 9:00 A.M.

OKLAHOMA
Station - KAAY - 1090 KC
Sunday 10:30 P.M.

OREGON
Station - KFAX - 1100 KC
Saturday 11:30 A.M.

PENNSYLVANIA
Philadelphia - WHAT - 1340 KC
Sunday 8:30 P.M.

Pittsburgh - WAMO - FM - 105.9 MHZ
Sunday 11:30 A.M.

RHODE ISLAND
Providence - WRYT - 950 KC
Sunday 3:00 P.M.

SOUTH CAROLINA
St. George - WQIZ - 810 KC
Sunday 2:45 P.M.

Winnsboro - WCKM - 1250 KC
Sunday 8:30 A.M.

Florence - WYNN - 540 KC
Sunday 1:30 P.M.

TENNESSEE
Knoxville - WJBE - 1430 KC
Sunday 8:30 A.M.

Memphis - WDIA - 1270 KC
Sunday 12:00 P.M.

TEXAS
Houston - KCOH - 1430 KHZ
Sunday 8:30 A.M.

Station - KAAY - 1090 KC
Sunday 10:30 P.M.

VERMONT
Station - WRYT - 950 KC
Sunday 3:00 P.M.

VIRGINIA
Norfolk - WRAP - 850 KC
Sunday 9:00 A.M.

Richmond - Petersburg - Williamsburg - WENZ - 1450KHZ
Sunday 8:00 A.M.

WASHINGTON, D.C.
Station - WEBB - 1360 KC
Sunday 10:30 A.M.

Station - WOL - AM - 1450
Sunday 10:30 A.M.

STATE OF WASHINGTON
Station - KFAX - 1100 KC
Saturday 11:30 A.M.

OVERSEAS STATIONS

HONOLULU * HAWAII
Station - KORL - 650 KHZ
Sunday 12:00 P.M.

CARIBBEAN ISLANDS
BARBADOS
ST. CROIX
ST. JOHN
ST. THOMAS
TORTOLA
VIRGIN ISLANDS
Station - WSTX - AM 930
Sunday 7:00 A.M.

ANGUILLA
ANEGADA
SOMBREROL
VIRGIN GORDA
TORTOLA
ST. CROIX
ST. JOHN
ST. MARTIN
SABA
ST. BARTHELEMY
ST. EUSTATIUS
ST. CHRISTOPHER
NEVIS
MONTSERRAT
ANTIGUA
BARBUDA
Radio Anguilla - 1505 KC
Sunday 9:30 P.M.

BERMUDA
Station ZFB - AM. 960KHZ
FM. 94.9 MGA
Sunday 8:30 P.M.

WORLD-WIDE RADIO
Radio Station WGCB - Short Wave Receiver
15.185mgz - 17.720mgz
EVERY WEDNESDAY AT 5:00 P.M.
NEW YORK TIME
EUROPE - NORTH ATLANTIC - AFRICA - SOUTH PACIFIC - SOUTH AMERICA - FAR EAST - CANADA NEAR EAST - CENTRAL AMERICA - CARIBBEAN

REACHING 1 HALF BILLION PEOPLE WEEKLY

Deliverance Evangelistic Centers
Weekly Schedule Of Services...

Brooklyn Deliverance
Evangelistic Center—Tabernacle
785 DeKalb Avenue
Brooklyn, N.Y. 11221

Newark Deliverance National Headquarters & Temple
10th Street & Clinton Avenue * Newark, New Jersey 07108

Philadelphia Deliverance Evangelistic
Center—Tabernacle
60th St & Lansdowne Avenue
Phila, Pa 19151

NEWARK

MONDAY 7:30pm Charismatic Deliverance Soul Winner's Bible Institute
TUESDAY 7:00pm Supernatural Anointing Service
Evangelist Arturo Skinner, Administering
FRIDAY 8:00pm Great Holy Ghost Rallies
SUNDAY
12:00 noon Sunday School
3:00pm Great Supernatural Healing Service
Evangelist Arturo Skinner, Administering

BROOKLYN

SATURDAY 2:30pm Supernatural Healing Service
Evangelist Arturo Skinner, Administering
SUNDAY 9:00am Sunday School
11:00am Morning Worship
THURSDAY 8:00pm Great Holy Ghost Rallies

PHILADELPHIA

SUNDAY 10:45am Supernatural Anointing Service
Evangelist Arturo Skinner, Administering

Application to mail at 2nd. Class postage rates
is pending at Brooklyn, N.Y.

PERSONALITY AND CONSECRATION

The powerful ministry of deliverance cannot be separated from the larger-than-life personality of Apostle Skinner. It is said that God can work through personality or despite personality. His extravagant personality existed before his own salvation. During his time in show business, he maintained a very well-furnished home. He always emphasized the importance of being well-groomed and kempt. His suits were pressed and neat without a hair on his head being out of place. He expected those around him to be the same way. Former publicist, Bishop Wayne Johnson, explained the following:

> If you didn't really know him it would just seem that he was moody. But he was really just sensitive spiritually. You figure he was receiving prophetic words, unctions and words of knowledge for dozens of people in a meeting. He had a lot on him and sometimes it made him grumpy from feeling so much. It became difficult to decipher what was his burden versus someone else's. Or what was his own illness versus someone else's that he felt for them.[18]

Skinner was known for his loving and paternal nature. He protected everyone connected to him and expressed his love often. He believed strongly in caring for the "fatherless" in accordance with the Scriptures. Apostle Skinner adopted many of the young people in the church who didn't have fathers in their lives, providing for them out of his own pockets. Of his benevolent nature, Congressman John Rooney said, "Through his efforts and those of his constituent congregations, many hundreds of students are helped to obtain college educations. More than 3,000 persons are helped each week—many of whom are dope addicts, alcoholics, and derelicts from all walks of life. Such help is focused on attaining continuous rehabilitation and employment."[19]

He gave Christmas gifts, paid for school and many other things for the youth in his church. While loving, he was also very protective. If he felt anyone was trying to take advantage of God's people, especially his youth, his admonishment was unflinching. He was very direct and blunt in his speech, often correcting toxic behaviors over the pulpit or confronting the person directly. He strongly believed in walking in truth and transparency, shunning the very appearance of evil and deception. He continued this same direct and blunt approach even in his relationships with other ministers. This wasn't always well-received and put him at odds with them very often. . "He often felt like his enemy was to be everyone's enemy also and this often created problems," Bishop Johnson said.[20]

For Skinner, the ministry of the supernatural was to be guarded.

was not just another church to Apostle Skinner. Deliverance was a place where God manifested himself in signs and wonders, making His presence known. Therefore, it was to be guarded with great reverence. The signs and wonders were signs of the tangible presence of God and therefore ministry was to be handled with great care. Skinner's strong personality was not reserved to just pastoring his members at Deliverance. It bled over into his other relationships and sometimes caused him to be at odds with others that he felt were not doing the right thing.

Skinner never married. He would often jokingly state in his corporate prayers, "I thank you once, I thank you twice for my intended wife." His stance did not detract women from seeking to be Mrs. Skinner. One particular woman went as far as wearing a wedding dress to the church. "Although Apostle Skinner wasn't harshly against the idea, the Mothers in the church especially disapproved of it. They felt it would be a distraction for him from doing ministry unhindered," Bishop Johnson explained.[21] Skinner often looked to the Mothers in the church for accountability, rebuke, and guidance to help keep him on the right path.

DEATH AND LEGACY

By 1975, Apostle Skinner had run several successful conferences at Madison Square Garden and other large arenas. He also conducted crusades across the country evangelizing the sinner and empowering the saints. The fellowship had churches across the country and even in other countries. At the same time, Apostle Skinner's health was declining. The biggest challenge to those who are mightily used of God is self-care and rest. It is said of many of the evangelists and crusaders such as Jack Coe, A.A. Allen, and William Branham that their health concerns came from exhaustion and lack of rest. It is believed that the work of ministry took its toll on Apostle Skinner. Skinner was slowly beginning to appear less and less at the church. He remained in his home, ill, while two ministers at the church continued to preach and run services.[22] He made one final appearance at a Tuesday night service and fell into a coma shortly after. He went to be with the Lord suddenly on March 20, 1975, after succumbing to an unknown illness. His funeral service was jam packed with his members and admirers from near and far. Eventually, the Brooklyn church closed down, its building sold, and attention was given to the Newark church under the leadership of Bishop Ralph Nichol.

The impact of Apostle Arturo Skinner cannot be measured in this chapter alone. Skinner laid a foundation for those that followed him. He was like a forerunner for many other black ministers. As the forerunner, his ministry affected both of the other figures featured in this reading, Mosley and Washington. Skinner blazed a trail of the supernatural in the ministry that hundreds of other ministers have walked through and continue to walk through. His apostleship would be defined by being deployed by God to bring the demonstrative ministry of the Spirit to the black community. In many ways, Skinner took the black church beyond the Baptism of the Holy Ghost and sanctification. Through his ministry, for example, divine healing was no longer restricted to the traveling Evangelist's tent. Altar calls were no longer exclusive to salvation for sinners but empowerment for Believers as well. These things must be credited to the laboring of Apostle Arturo Skinner.

---

2 Blocker, James. Yours Because of Calvary: The Life and Times of Apostle Arturo A. Skinner. Maitland, Florida: Xulon Press, 2013. Pg. 258.

3 Synan, Vinson. The Holiness-Pentecostal Tradition: Charismatic Movements in the Twentieth Century. Grand Rapids: Erdmans, 1997. Pg. 2230.

4 Blocker, Yours Because of Calvary, 384.

5 Taylor, Clarence. The Black Churches of Brooklyn. New York: Columbia University Press, 1996. Pg. 51-52.

6 COGIC Publishing Board, COGIC Manual. Memphis: Self-Publish, 1973. Pg. 141.

7 Assembly of God, 26-27 Minutes of the 23rd General Council of the Assemblies of God.

8 Eckhardt, John. Moving in the Apostolic. Bloomington, MN: Chosen Books, 1999. Pg. 19-21.

9 COGIC Manual, 134.

10 Blocker, Yours Because of Calvary, 423.

11 Pastor Gilbert White (former Deliverance member). Phone interview with the author. October 17, 2020.

12 Skinner, Arturo. 9 Gifts of the Spirit. Brooklyn, NY: Deliverance Evangelistic Center, 1975. Pg. 23.

13 Taylor, The Black Churches of Brooklyn, Pg. 50.

14 Synan, Vinson. The Century of the Holy Spirit: 100 Years of Pentecostal and Charismatic Renewal. Nashville: Thomas Nelson 2001. Pg. 283.

15 Deliverance Voice, 1971.

16 Ibid.

17 Skinner, 9 Gifts of the Spirit, Pg. 8.

18 Bishop Wayne Johnson (former publicist), Phone interview with the author, January 7, 2021.

19 Hon. John Rooney, Extension of Remarks, Congressional Record, Thursday, July 8, 1971, e7308.

20 Johnson, Phone interview with the author.

21 Bishop Wayne Johnson (former publicist), Phone Interview with the Author, January 7, 2021.

22 Blocker, Yours Because of Calvary, 1334.

APOSTLE JOHNNIE WASHINGTON

When we think of megachurches we imagine the sprawling, mammoth-sized ministries that often purchased old malls and department stores for their sanctuaries. We saw a wave of "mega mania" in the 1990s and 2000s, bringing to the forefront churches such as West Angeles, New Birth, The Potter's House, and many others. Their refined, family-friendly, and punctual culture revolutionized how the local church was presented and perceived. Megachurches typically thrive in more suburban areas, especially in the south. They are not common in the urban community or "hood" these days, but that was certainly not always the case.

The concept of "mega-ministry" is hardly new at all. In the late 1970s and 80s, Tabernacle of Prayer for All People, The Center of Hope, was lifting a sound out of Queens, New York that traveled around the nation. Tabernacle added an evangelistic edge to the local church experience powerfully interweaving the zeal of revival with the structure of an organized church. The impact of the Tabernacle cannot be separated from their leader whose dual ministry on the street corner and in the pulpit left an indelible impression on the saved and unsaved alike. His name was

Apostle Johnnie Washington.

Johnnie Lee Washington was born in Mt. Bayou, Mississippi on March 3, 1929. He and his parents attended a local Baptist church. He was largely raised by his grandmother but was sent back to his parents after her passing. From an early age, young Johnnie expressed a keen interest in faith and the supernatural. He often found himself drawn to supernatural experiences and churches that were expressive about the power of God. His education was scarce as he often had to devote himself to helping his family.

Johnnie found solace in singing and did so to express his devotion to God. He moved to New Orleans to further pursue his career. While there, he joined a singing group that was preparing to do residency in New York City for a month. Without giving it much thought, he quit his job and went to New York. After the month-long residence was over, young Johnnie decided to stay and later joined another group, the Gospel Wonders. The group's popularity caused them to travel quite a bit, even crossing paths with Little Richard after he briefly left secular music. But their popularity in gospel music was not a reflection of their commitment to the Gospel, according to Washington. The tension came to a head for young

Johnnie when they toured the Mid-west.

He found himself stuck between the powerfully enlightening experiences in church and the wild, quenching reality of the world around him. This had been a repeated theme in his life since childhood where he saw "saints" rejoice in church one way and live totally different afterward. After becoming exhausted with the up and down of the group, he shut up himself in his hotel room for a few days, refusing to leave or to continue the tour. He went back to New York without the group, seeking answers from God on what to do. He saw a vision on that bus that changed his life in that moment. "There appeared a great mass choir, with the women dressed in black skirts and white blouses. The men were in black trousers and white shirts. I was standing in front of the choir in an auditorium as their director."[1]

Johnnie returned to New York determined to live for God. He joined St. Mary Church of Christ, Disciples of Christ in Brooklyn, New York under Bishop James Gardener. After joining, he fell ill and developed gangrene on his leg. While awaiting amputation, the Lord spoke to him and told him to go to the church. When he got there, Bishop Gardener laid hands on him and prayed for God to heal him. When he awoke the next day, the gangrene was miraculously gone! This experience would shape the remainder of Johnnie's ministry. Although not strongly cessationist, the Disciples of Christ were not major supporters of supernatural gifts and experiences. Though they didn't always discourage it, it was not seen as a common occurrence in the church.

Washington committed himself to the church and led the organization's Northeastern choir. He asked himself if this could be the choir that he saw on the bus. Within a short time, he found that the choir's behavior didn't quite match what he had seen in his vision. Yet he kept trying to get them there. But when a choir member received healing after Washington laid hands on him, the entire choir changed. After this, miracles became weekly occurrences for the group. Their rehearsals became mini-services. Each of the choir members developed stronger commitments to salvation, much to Johnnie's excitement.

Soon after, he accepted the call to preach at the church. His pulpit of choice: the street corner. Positioned on Fulton and Franklin Avenue in Brooklyn, New York he raised his voice, preaching to whoever would hear him. Washington had a strong passion for evangelism and street ministry. His message was an unflinching, fire-and-brimstone call to

"Holiness." It was often met with mockery, spitting, and cursing from those who heard it. But Minister Washington was unmoved. He established a church with the Disciples of Christ in Red Hook, a neighborhood in East Brooklyn. Though he was with the Disciples of Christ, Washington employed elements that were typical to Pentecostal worship: tambourines, handclapping, foot-stomping, shut-ins, and more. He decided to leave his denomination and the church to focus on his street ministry. "I was not exactly sad about this since this would leave me free to travel and bring the Gospel to the field...I was just as happy on the street corner. I was just as at home on the street corner preaching as I was in a pulpit."[2]

In 1969, Washington was called back to another church with which he had fellowshipped to become its pastor. He agreed hesitantly and the congregation restarted in a small mission in Brooklyn. Despite his reservations, the Lord gave him a name, "Tabernacle of Prayer for All People, the Center of Hope," named after the Scripture in Matthew 21:13 where Jesus declared that His Father's house was a house of prayer for all people. Another stipulation before he agreed was that there needed to be a commitment to holiness. By definition, Apostle Washington stated,

"The church would be different. No selling, buying, anniversaries, appreciations, baby rallies, waist rallies, jewelry, make-up or any other such thing. We would be sanctified and holy."[3]

Surprisingly, the people agreed to the standards and the work began. Soon after he began pastoring, the church outgrew the building and had to find another. Within another two years, they had to find another larger building as the growth continued. One of their reasons for growth was their strong evangelistic outreach to the community. Reverend Washington set up a tent on Eastern Parkway and Hopkinson in Brooklyn over an abandoned lot. Here, he preached the Gospel, evangelized the corners, and ministered deliverance in these powerful services. Washington said:

> The tent ministry is my heart and could not be rivaled by anything else I did for the Lord. I was simply happiest when my feet were on the sawdust trail. The only thing that concerned me were those souls—those hungry souls who would come hear the saving message of the Gospel. There were times I felt that God did not give anyone else charge of the tent ministry except me."[4]

The tent was no different than the brick-and-mortar. Signs and wonders were reported regularly under the tent too. By the time their tent revivals were over, hundreds more came to join the church. Tabernacle needed another building and a much bigger one this time. Planning began for another facility where they could worship. They found a building that was out of their normal price range but they were determined to claim it. He was adamantly against all kinds of fundraising such as dinner sales or unorthodox rallies that other churches would employ. If they were going to get this property, it would be through what he considered, "God's way of raising money—tithes and offerings."

They purchased a former synagogue and occupied it right afterwards, but this one was a little too big. The building sat 1,200 people, whereas the other ones only sat in the hundreds. The empty seats only fueled Reverend Washington to work harder in his evangelistic ministry. He began running revivals in New York, New Jersey, and even in states beyond that. Before long, the 1,200-seat building was too small as well.

In addition to the tent revivals and Sunday service, Reverend Washington also started a Bible institute as a place where people could come and "learn the Word of God." One author wrote that Bible institutes serve "as a protest to the inroads of secularization in higher education and as a base for the education of lay workers and full-time Bible teachers, evangelists, and pastors."[5] Most Pentecostals and Charismatics didn't believe in formal, theological education since much of the critical methods of handling the Bible were considered offensive, blasphemous, and contrary to belief in the Bible being the "inspired and only infallible written Word of God." Bible schools and institutes would further counteract this secularizing tendency and encourage Bible literacy while maintaining their zeal for the Holy Spirit.

Tabernacle's Bible Institute was headed by Dr. C.R. Johnson, a formally educated man with a keen knowledge of the Scriptures. Originally, they operated as an extension of the noted Manhattan Bible Institute in Harlem. Tabernacle's advantage was that it was the first of its kind in Brooklyn and serviced those in the local community. Eventually its reach went far beyond Brooklyn. The school boasted strong administration and insightful Bible teaching that was hard to beat. They hosted Tuesday night chapel services weekly and soon attendees packed out the 1,200-seat auditorium. It was time to seek another building. What they would find would change their ministry forever.

THE MIRACLE ON JAMAICA AVENUE

Apostle Washington had begun looking for theatres where his large congregation could continue to grow comfortably. Loew's had a series of theatres throughout New York City that had been discontinued once multi-screen theatres came into play. Churches had begun buying them, such as Reverend Ike in Harlem with the Paradise Theatre and Apostle Skinner in Brooklyn with Kismet Theatre. One theatre that he had set his eyes on in Brooklyn had just been sold to someone else by Mr. Mateo. He was wholly committed to keeping his congregation in Brooklyn where he had worked intensely in evangelistic ministry for so long. One night he was contacted by Mr. Mateo and offered another building in Jamaica, Queens, which he initially declined. Apostle Washington recounted the story in his memoir, Lord, Why Me: The Making of an Apostle. "He told me to hear him out, 'Reverend, before you hang up, I think you should know that I do not want to sell you this theater, I want to give it to you.' I jumped straight up in the bed and asked him where he was. I had determined that wherever he was, I would meet him as quickly as possible."[6]

The theatre was originally called the Valencia Theatre and was a major entertainment hub for Queens in the 1920s and 30s. The theater itself was part of a series of "Wonder Theatres," named so for their notable pipe organs created by Robert Morton Wonder. Eventually, many of the "Wonder Theatres" began closing down as they were replaced by multi-room theatres that are more common today. Although they were no longer relevant for movies, these illustrious theatres became ideal places for thriving churches. These theatres were purchased or donated to mostly black churches across the city. Apostle Washington was among the first of many pastors that expanded into these facilities. Eventually, Loew's Gates Theatre became the Pilgrim Renaissance Convention Center. The Normandy Theatre became Pleasant Grove Tabernacle in Brooklyn.

To serve as collateral, the church gave Mr. Loew $1 for the former Valencia Theatre in Jamaica, Queens and the rest is history.7 The transition was not smooth. The church had to do major work to the building to transform it into what it is today. But the Tabernacle was largely self-contained. They worked together to build their own seats from scratch, paint, and clean the building. The New York Times described the architecture of the building as a Parisian theme with hints of Mexican-American design:

The vast auditorium itself will make even the most jaded architectural pilgrim gasp, or even kneel. The room is ringed by high walls, statues, parapets and towers, asymmetrically arranged and all elaborately baroque. The proscenium arch is formed by a succession of statuary niches. But the ceiling is completely plain, a sky blue—as if the auditorium is a courtyard open to the sky.[8]

For the members of the Tabernacle, this was simply the beauty of holiness and added to the vastness and loftiness of the God they served. In October 1977, the church dedicated the 3,500 seat Valencia Theatre and converted it into the Tabernacle of Prayer for All People. In Apostle Washington's words, "Not one chicken dinner sold, waist rally, or anything else like that." The empty seats in the Tabernacle served as motivation for evangelism and crusading. And with 3,500 seats, Apostle Washington and the church could not hit the streets fast enough.

THE TABERNACLE EXPERIENCE

In the late 1970s and 80s, the Pentecostal experience was beginning to evolve. Preachers in bigger churches traded their spirited delivery for a more direct and practical teaching style. Their choirs would lift a friendly number or nothing at all. The worship broadcasted on television at that time presented a more refined image of Pentecostals. "These leaders also introduced a preaching style that countered the homiletic practices of the sanctified church model in which they stressed instruction rather than inspiration."[9] Whereas some churches were formalized while in their building and radical on the streets, Tabernacle treated their gatherings like weekly revivals. Thousands gathered weekly to have the Tabernacle experience.

Needless to say, the vision Washington had as a young man was manifested. Every week, the 300-voice Tabernacle choir mounted the stand in their black and white to lift their voices with their anthems, hymns, or original material. The choir was so large that only the women were on the actual choir stand and the men stood on the floor facing the director. Their selections were often followed up with explosive dancing, shouting, and rejoicing common to the Pentecostal experience. The 3,500-seat theatre would be filled with the sound of driving organ, thumping drums, rolling percussion, popping tambourines, double clapping, and foot stomping. Tabernacle would sometimes erupt in praise so strongly, there was no sermon. In this, they pointed to 2 Chronicles 5:14: "So that the priests could not stand to minister by reason of the cloud: for

Apostle Washington explained, "Praise is common among the saints of God. The spirit of healing moves when one praises. Praising and singing edifies the soul, it brings joy to the soul of the individual...you can get more from praising God than begging."[10]

Mass communication theory in a religious context would suggest that with a crowd this large, you'd want to keep your message simple, light-hearted, and even entertaining. But Apostle Washington's preaching ministry was different. He said, "[I was told] no one would want to listen to me...I kept maintaining through the Holy Ghost that there had to be a difference between holiness and unholiness. I insisted that we look different, talk different, dress different, act different and above all, live holy and love the Lord with all our hearts...They thought I should lighten up, but the devil is a liar!"[11] His message of holiness demanded cutting and direct truth, no matter who it offended. For Apostle Washington, offense was a birth pang that produced spiritual fruit. In this we see Apostle Washington's rejection of the "double life" that he saw often as a young boy and a gospel singer. Holiness required an absolute approach because God was absolutely holy. Correction and church discipline were an important part of keeping the house of God sacred and revered.

At the same time, Washington would often weep during altar calls as he preached and compelled sinners to come, feeling burdened for their condition. His preaching also corrected Believers into being more aware and discerning. He outwardly condemned predatory schemes used by questionable preachers such as telling people to give their rent money to the evangelist for a special blessing or buying blessed soaps, oils, and other fraudulent products. He advocated the use of wisdom and discernment throughout the body of Christ.

At the same time, signs and wonders were as much a part of the service as sober preaching. In some interpretations of the spiritual gifts in 1 Corinthians 12, "power gifts" are reserved for winning sinners to Christ. But at Tabernacle, power and demonstration were not confined exclusively to the tent meeting or evangelistic crusade. In an interview, Washington stated, "A revival is a time when the people come in to worship and praise God and be revived in their strength and their teaching. Many times revival is for the saints. Crusades are for the sinners, revival is for the saints."[12]

Further, every service was treated like there were those in the congregation who needed to be saved. There was always an altar call for salvation made for the people. The altar was considered very sacred and important to their service. "The Lord spoke and said that our altar calls were like a delivery room experience...Therefore when a soul is born into the Kingdom of God, it is the church that becomes the delivery room. We who are already saved, are there to assist in the delivery with our praises. Instead of encouraging the mother to push, we encourage the souls at the altar to praise God knowing he will enter into a heart that is filled with praises of Him."[1]

As a result, the demonstration of the Spirit and power was a major part of this appeal to the sinner. At the back of the church one could find canes, crutches, back braces, wheelchairs and more that served as reminders to the church about the miracles in the lives of the people to whom he had ministered. A sermon could easily be interrupted with the question, "How long have you been in this condition?" as he discerned an affliction in a person's body and prepared to pray for them.

In Tabernacle, the laying on of hands was not confined to healing and miracles, he also laid hands as a charge of empowerment and stirring for Believers. Apostle Washington reflected on one of these services toward the end of his life: "I stood to make the appeal for the broadcast offering and general offering, but the Holy Ghost said to me, 'Minister.' I began to call people out of the audience and pray for them and God just began to slay people in the Spirit."[13]

As he continued to minister, the crowds continued to come from near and far. Eventually, Apostle Washington established a fellowship of Tabernacle churches that spread across the country and abroad. In 1978 alone, there were over 20 "Tabernacles of Prayer" spread across the country. The largest was in Goldsboro, North Carolina where Apostle Washington held revival meetings even before the church was established. The fellowship came together often for what they called "Deeper Life Conferences" and other gatherings. However, the apex of the Tabernacle movement was their grand "Pentecost Sunday" celebrations. These events were as largely important as Easter Sunday. Prior to Apostle Washington, few protestants celebrated it as it was a major Sunday on the Catholic and Anglican calendars.

Pentecost Sunday was of major importance to Apostle Washington and the church. Pentecostals believe the Baptism of the Holy Ghost as a separate experience from conversion or getting saved. Members were asked to consecrate for 50 days leading up to it with different fasting times and procedures being set across those days. The weekend of Pentecost was a gathering complete with communion and feet washing on Friday and Saturday. On Pentecost Sunday, everyone gathered together in white, including the fellowship churches from other states. "If you got to church at 11:00 a.m., you were late and were going to have a hard time finding a seat," recounted Samuel Guillame, Tabernacle church historian.[14] "Buses would be lined up all down Jamaica Avenue." The atmosphere would be saturated with more than 3,500 people expecting a move of the Holy Spirit just as at the Upper Room; and they were never disappointed. Archbishop E. Bernard Jordan, a former member of Tabernacle, recalled, "Women would cover their heads with white head coverings for the duration of the fast.

But on that 50th day of Pentecost, we would come together and the women would take off the head coverings and twirl them in the air. The men would take out their white handkerchiefs and wave them. And the atmosphere would just be charged up with the power of God."[15]

Their celebrations soon became a citywide trend as many other churches caught on and continued the practice of celebrating Pentecost Sunday. Without a doubt, Tabernacle was making its mark. Within a few years, they owned the property across the street for their Bible School. Here students were instructed in the Word of God on Tuesdays and Thursdays. Programs included: New Testament Studies, Christian workers training, General Bible, Teacher's Training, Post-Graduate studies, as well as English and Reading, most of the courses being 2-year programs.[16] Their Bible school was just as important to their church culture as their crusades.

To maintain unity, the church boasted very few auxiliaries and no department heads or presidents. Apostle Washington served as the head of all ministries with everyone working on the same level with one another. According to him, this helped the church avoid politics and power trips among the members of the church.

In 1982, Apostle Washington teamed up with Apostles Jasper Rolle of Bronx, N.Y., Lobias Murray of Dallas, Charles O. Miles of Michigan, and others to host a conference called "The Apostles Council." Together they convened to address the state of the Church and discuss pertinent issues to the ministry. Washington was against denominationalism and sectarianism, once saying, "I wish I could take the names off every church building!" Anyone who preached holiness was a fellow laborer to him.

Cry Aloud

CIRCULATION 50,000   VOL. I NO. 1

"ALL THE CHURCH IS A PACIFIER"

You Must Read This Holy Ghost-filled message by Apostle Washington

oud

SUMMER 1978

A PUBLICATION OF TABERNACLE OF PRAYER FOR ALL PEOPLE INC.

- **EDITOR IN CHIEF — PASTOR**
  Apostle Johnnie Washington
- **ASST. PASTOR — COLUMNIST**
  Rev. C. R. Johnson
- **EDITOR**
  Sis. Faye L. Carson
- **MANAGING EDITOR — DESIGN**
  Bro. Alfred Simmons
- **PRODUCTION**
  Rev. Leon Bonner
  Sis. Catherine Loadholt
  Sis. Cynthia Hedgepeth

CRY ALOUD is a publication of the Tabernacle of Prayer For All People, Inc., 165-11 Jamaica Ave., Jamaica, New York 11432, and mailing address at P.O. Box 153, Brooklyn, N.Y. 11233. A religious, non-profit, non-stock corporation. A purely religious organization established by the laws of the State of New York.

Each gift from each donor is used as designated with the understanding that when any given need has been met, designated gifts may then be used where needed most.

EDITORIAL ... ALFRED SIMMONS

Because a man has seen the condition of the church, and because he is convinced that it is not God's will that His people should be bewildered, perplexed, and discouraged, he has made himself available to God. He has been charged to "Cry Aloud" against the causes of this condition, regardless of what they may be.

God has so honored the dedication and consecration, that an atmosphere for the Holy Spirit's moving has been created, and men and women are literally running from under their physical afflictions. They're throwing away their crutches and are dancing and leaping for joy. Drug addicts are being cleansed from their cursed habits without going through the failing treatments of men. Sinners by the scores are coming to Christ. Believers are learning how to trust the Lord for themselves and to stand on God's promises. Surely God is in the midst of us; filling the hungry with the Holy Ghost (in one recent evening service 57 people were filled with the Holy Ghost). Many who had never let loose and moved in the Spirit are now rejoicing and dancing in the freedom of the Holy Ghost. The eyes of the believers are opening to the lateness of the hour and they're being provoked into "being about their fathers business." Sloathful saints and dormant gifts are stirring into action. Associate ministers and missionaries are going around the world preaching and teaching the word of God. The young people are diligently going to the streets with tracts and literature. Only heaven will reveal the results of this ministry where hundreds of saints and sinners, who were discouraged and disenchanted, have found new inspiration, new life and a new desire to be in the center of God's will. If in less than eight years such a towering ministry has developed, we're convinced that *EYE HATH NOT SEEN, NOR EAR HEARD NEITHER HAVE ENTERED INTO THE HEART OF MAN, THE THINGS WHICH GOD HATH PREPARED FOR THEM THAT LOVE HIM*.

We Believe...

1. In the verbal inspiration of the Bible.
2. In one God eternally existing in three persons; namely the Father, Son, and Holy Ghost.
3. That Jesus Christ is the only begotten Son of the Father, conceived of the Holy Ghost, and born of the virgin Mary. That Jesus was crucified, buried, and raised from the dead; that He ascended to heaven and is today at the right hand of the Father as the Intercessor.
4. That all have sinned and come short of the glory of God, and that repentance is commanded by God for all and necessary for forgiveness of sins.
5. That justification, regeneration, and the new birth are wrought by faith in the blood of Jesus Christ.
6. In sanctification subsequent to the new birth, through faith in the blood of Christ; through the Word, and by the Holy Ghost.
7. Holiness to be God's standard of living for His people.
8. In the baptism of the Holy Ghost subsequent to a clean heart.
9. In speaking with other tongues as the Spirit gives utterance, and that is the initial evidence of the baptism of the Holy Ghost.
10. In water baptism by immersion, and all who repent should be baptized in the name of the Father, and of the Son, and of the Holy Ghost.
11. Divine healing is provided for all in the atonement.
12. In the Lord's Supper and washing of the saint's feet.
13. In the premillennial second coming of Jesus. First, to resurrect the righteous dead and to catch away the living saints to Him in the air. Second, to reign on the earth a thousand years.
14. In the bodily resurrection; eternal life for the righteous and eternal punishment for the wicked.

"All they get is a pacifier"

BY APOSTLE JOHNNIE WASHINGTON

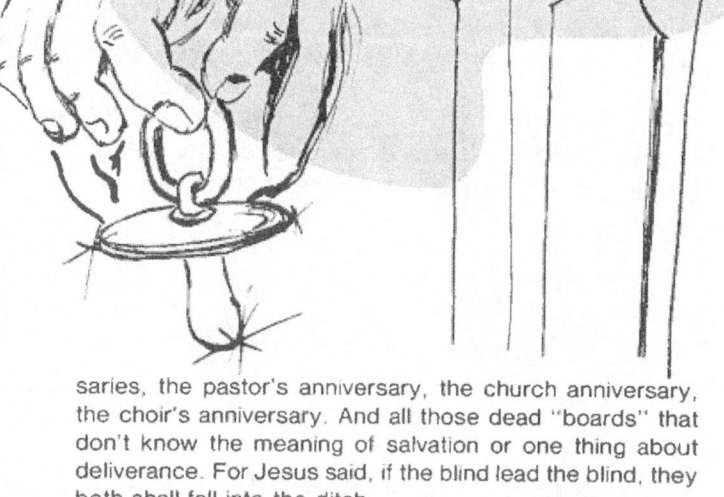

Jeremiah 23:1-2

"Woe unto the pastors who destroy and scatter the sheep of my pasture!" saith the Lord. Therefore, thus saith the Lord God of Israel, against the pastors who feed my people, Ye have scattered my flock, and driven them away, and have not visited them; behold, I will visit upon you the evil of your doings, saith the Lord."

Here God is expressing his anger towards the false preachers, teachers and pastors. God recognizes the needs of his people and understands that those needs are not being met.

Month after month, week after week, thousands around the world, (men, women, boys and girls) gather in meeting places expecting to be fed. To their injury, instead of being fed, they are only pacified. How disappointing for those precious hungry souls!

On one ocassion, Jesus asked Peter a question, "Peter do you love me?" His answer was, "Yes, Lord." Jesus replied, "Feed my lambs" Again he asks Peter, do you love me? Peter responded, "Yes Lord." Jesus responded, "Feed my sheep". Jesus asked the third time, "Peter, do you love me?" Following Peter's affirmation the Master exhorted him to feed his sheep. Jesus knew that if the sheep, who were able to look out for themselves, were not being fed, the poor lambs must be starving to death.

God has always desired that His people be properly fed, and that they prosper in health even as their souls prosper. For Jesus said that man shall not live by bread alone, but by every word that proceedeth out of the mouth of God. The church of today has lost its way and has caused millions of souls to be wondering from place to place, hoping, looking and begging for food, which is the Word of God. But as thousands fill the cushioned pews in their beautiful edifices, with stained glass windows, what do they get? A dry, dead message with no life, no healing, no deliverance. Those preachers who went and were not sent were mere pacifiers. Without much effort, they try to fill the longing needs of those hungry souls with quartet programs, bazaars, bingo games, chicken dinners, door knob rallies, fashion shows, and rock concerts. And please let us not forget those favorite pasttimes, anniversaries, the pastor's anniversary, the church anniversary, the choir's anniversary. And all those dead "boards" that don't know the meaning of salvation or one thing about deliverance. For Jesus said, if the blind lead the blind, they both shall fall into the ditch.

How sad it must make God, when He sees thousands of His children, along with their pastors and bishops, filling the doctors' offices and hospitals, when God has spoken in Exodus 15:26, "I am the Lord that healeth thee."

Now may I ask you a question? IS THERE ANYTHING TOO HARD FOR GOD? When the gospel is preached in its fullness, men and women, boys and girls will be saved, healed, delivered and set free from the powers of satan. But the *gospel* must be preached in order to see these Holy Ghost, supernatural transformations. Through preaching, the gospel of faith is built up in the hearts of believers, "For faith cometh by hearing, and hearing by the Word of God." Rom 10:17

One of the biggest words in the English language is IF. "If I be lifted up from the earth, I will draw all men unto me." 2nd Chronicles 14:7 says, "If my people which are called by my name shall humble themselves and pray, and seek my face, and turn from their wicked ways; then will I hear from heaven, and will forgive their sin, and will heal their land."

Those who attend the modern church today are just like babies sucking on rubber nipples; when there is no fluid left in the bottle, he only fills himself with air. That is why you see, so many people today, who claim to be Christians, just shooting off hot air. For if they had been fed and not pacified, the result would have been a Holy, dedicated, consecrated, fully yielded life. But the old pacifier (the false preacher) feeds the people numbers, blessing plans, sweet smelling oils, candles, and all kinds of tricks, dreamed up by the devil, which amounts to hot air from a nipple that is connected to nothing. God's word tells us that we should know the truth and the truth shall set us free. 2nd Timothy 2:15 says, "Study to show thyself approved unto God, a workman that needeth not to be ashamed, rightly dividing the word of truth."

In the book of Leviticus, 19:31, we are told not to regard the spiritualist, or the witch or the wizards for they all are motivated by the power of satan. For Romans 16:17-18 says, "Now I beseech you bretheren, mark them which cause divisions and offenses contrary to the doctrine which ye have learned; and avoid them For they that are such, serve not our Lord Jesus Christ but their own bellies and by good words and fair speeches deceive the hearts of the simple."

Those who have never had the word of God hidden in their hearts have only been sucking on a pacifier. But God is speaking to the preacher, woe unto you who are causing souls to go to hell because you are not preaching the gospel. God is speaking in the book of Joel 2:32, "And it shall come to past that whosoever shall call on the name of the Lord shall be delivered, for in Mt. Zion and in Jerusalem shall be deliverance, as the Lord hath said, and in the remnant who the Lord shall call."

Beloved, today I beg of you to come to Him now, for he is standing with outstretched hands, saying, "Come unto me all ye that labor and are heavy laden and I will give you rest."

Revelation 3:20 declares "Behold I stand at the door, and knock; if any man hear my voice and open the door, I will come in to him and will sup with him, and he with me."

God bless you! My earnest and sincere prayer is that God will provide direction in your life and grant you spiritual insight that you may know the difference between being pacified and satisfied. Then, and only then, can you feed your mind, heart and spirit on the word of God.

WHAT DOES IT MEAN TO BE BORN AGAIN?

The new birth is a creative act of the Holy Spirit. It is not reformation; it is transformation. It is an act of God whereby man's sin is washed in the blood of Jesus. When a man is born again, he is born of the spirit. Old things are passed away, behold all things become new. (2 Cor. 5:17)

Jesus Christ explains the new birth in John 3. He points out that he is not talking about a physical but a spiritual birth. You may be a partaker of this experience by:
1. ACKNOWLEDGING that you are a sinner. (Romans 3:23)
2. REPENTING of those sins. (Acts 3:19)
3. CONFESSING those sins to God. (1 Jon 1:9)
4. FORSAKING your sins. (Isaiah 55:7)
5. BELIEVING in the finished work of Calvary (John 3:16)
6. RECEIVING Jesus into your heart. (John 1:11-12)

WHY NOT MAKE THIS MOST IMPORTANT DECISION NOW? AND THEN WRITE TO US AND LET US CONTINUE TO PRAY FOR YOU.
WRITE TO: TABERNACLE OF PRAYER — P.O. BOX 153, BROOKLYN, N.Y 11233

I have followed the scriptural stairway that you have shown me, and I am now accepting Christ as my personal Saviour. Please continue to pray for me.

(PLEASE PRINT)   DATE _____

NAME _____   TEL. NO. _____

STREET _____ APT. NO. _____ CITY _____ STATE _____ ZIP _____

NEW BORN _____ RECLAIMED _____ BAPTISM OF THE HOLY SPIRIT _____ OTHER _____

TABERNACLE OF PRAYER FOR ALL PEOPLE, INC.

I AM ALREADY ON THE MAILING LIST ☐ YES   ☐ NO

THE PLACE TO GROW AS

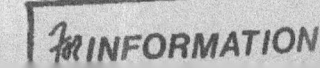

INFORMATION

WE'RE JUST BEGINNING...

August 1974 leaving 41 Rockaway Ave.

Marching to 503 Glenmore Ave.

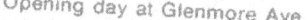

Opening day at Glenmore Ave.

503 Glenmore Ave. will long be remembered as a "Center of Hope".

Reverend Johnnie Washington, born and called by God to do a great work in the winning of souls, was ordained an Elder in the Gospel Ministry by the Church of Christ in September, 1967, under the Auspicies of the late Bishop W. C. Gilliam.

Having this great vision that God had given him, he continued his ministry as an evangelist on the field. With the scripture, Matthew 28:19-20, burning in his heart, and holding fast and faithfully to his calling, Reverend Washington began his very first revival. For five exciting, supernatural weeks, God opened the eyes of the blind, unstopped deaf ears, and set the captives free. With God moving in such a powerful way, he was called to Pastor a small mission in the Red Hook Section of Brooklyn.

About this time, God called him to Pastor another small mission on Rockaway Avenue in Brooklyn; and the two missions merged to become the first Tabernacle of Prayer for All People, Inc.

God so moved in this little mission, and filled the people there with such love and concern for fallen humanity, that in a matter of months the congregation grew so large it became necessary to move to larger quarters at 41 Rockaway Avenue, Brooklyn, New York. It was here, that God revealed His plan to his servant, Pastor Washington, that this ministry would be a ministry for all races, creeds, nationalities and religions. With this precious promise, Pastor Washington moved forward in the strength of God

Continued on following page... →

...and we're moving with God, expanding in the Spirit..and because of His promises...

One of the world's largest gospel tents attracts thou[sands]

The people are still hungry for the truth.

Jersey City Crusade... thousands are blessed & delivered as Apostle Washington crusades around country.

Pastor Washington speaks a word of knowledge.

Tent revival altar call... Thousands have come, but there's still room for more.

'78 T.B.I. Graduation class one of [the largest] bible institutes in N.Y. metropolita[n area]

with a double annointing of Holy Boldness. As this young man took his stand against sin, satan and the devil, God stood with him; and the ministry continued to grow.

In 1973, God broadened Pastor Washington's ministry; and a tent revival broke out in Brooklyn that can only be likened to the revival held in Nineveh.

In 1974, the Tabernacle Family moved to 503 Glenmore Avenue, Brooklyn, New York where God continued to save, set free, and deliver His people. 1976 saw God send Brooklyn another supernatural Tent Revival Crusade. In this revival, God moved by His Power. Over 2,000 souls were saved, hundreds baptized and filled with the Holy Spirit, and hundreds more were healed and delivered

Every week our family increases. Pastor Washington greets new members.

Dynamic Tabernacle Crusade Choir rings out "With Jesus Alone I'm Satisfied".

Elder C.R. Johnson, our anointed assistant pastor and dean of Tabernacle Bible Institute, exhorts crowd to praise the Lord.

Thousands continue to fill our Tabernacle to hear what thus saith the Lord.

there's more to come

June, 1977, the Big Gospel Tent was once again raised on a site in Brooklyn, New York. It was during this revival that ...oved upon the hearts of the executives of Loew's Corporation and caused them to donate the Valencia Theater located ...acia Avenue in Jamacia, New York to the Tabernacle of Prayer as a tax-free gift. Once again God has kept his promise ...den our borders and enable us to reach the multitudes with the message of the gospel of Jesus Christ.

October 16, 1977, after extensive rennovation, our new ediface was dedicated -- not by man but by the Holy Ghost. ...nds filled our auditorium to give God praises for what he had done. The new Tabernacle seats approxiamtely 4,000 ... Its Spanish decor, blinking stars, and intricate detailed structure gives it a unique atmosphere. Souls continue to be ...baptized and filled with the Holy Spirit, and set free as the power of God sweeps through the auditorium.

for we've only just begun

God said:

"...HE WAS WOUNDED FOR OUR TRANSGRESSIONS, HE WAS BRUISED FOR OUR INIQUITIES: THE CHASTISEMENT OF OUR PEACE WAS UPON HIM; AND WITH HIS STRIPES We Are Healed!"

FROM SUICIDE TO GREAT JOY

Moses Richardson

Last year I fell four floors down a shaft at the New York Post Office, 34th Street. I was unconscious for three and one-half hours. I was taken to the French Hospital on 33 Street. Doctors worked around the clock. I was confined to bed for 41 days with my left leg in traction and my right leg in traction. Both knees had to have cushions. My left eye was impaired and two fingers on the left side of my body were damaged.

Discouraged and depressed I decided to end my life but praise God, on my way I met some of the young people from Tabernacle of Prayer, who brought me to the service.

As I began to attend the services at Tabernacle of Prayer, the Lord saved me, baptized and filled me with the Holy Ghost and delivered me. I praise God for the power of the Holy Spirit.

Nervous Condition

Alfreda Thomas

In September, 1975, I began attending Tabernacle of Prayer. I had been under the doctor's care for a nervous condition since February of 1970. The doctor had told me that there was no cure for my condition and had placed me on various kinds of medication. By 1975 my condition had become more severe. I was unable to function on my job and was forced to take a medical leave of absence. At that time I had both a medical doctor and a psychiatrist. In spite of all this professional help, my condition continued to deteriorate.

Thank God that when I came to Tabernacle, the man of God called me out of the audience and told me that God wanted to deliver me and set me free. Praise God I was completely healed and set free. It has been more than two years now since I have had any medication. I am back on the job in perfect health both physically and mentally. God is a deliverer.

No More Fear!

Gloria Felder

I was bound by a spirit of fear for six years. During that time I was unable to leave my home. The fear was so severe that I couldn't even go across the street to the store. My husband had to do all the shopping. I sought help from various psychiatrist. They placed me on medication for five years, but the problem still was there.

Praise God, on July 26, 1976, God set me free. Now I am able to travel where ever I desire to go. There is no more fear in my life. Not only that, but I am no longer on medication. God delivered me from medication without any after effect. All praise and honor to God who has not given me the spirit of fear but of power, and of love, and of a sound mind.

From Drug Addiction to Holy Ghost Baptism

Montez Williams

On Sunday, June 12, I was unable to sleep. There was a desire within me to attend church with my sister. I got dressed and went to my sister's house. She brought me to the City-Wide Camp Meeting. During the service the Spirit of the Lord convicted my heart. That afternoon I received Jesus Christ as my personal Savior. The Lord delivered me and set me free from drug addiction, prostitution, lying, stealing, and all sin. I praise God for the power of the Holy Spirit that was demonstrated in my life. He continues to prove himself faithful to me. That same day the Lord baptised and filled me with the Holy Ghost. All the honor belongs to the Lord.

Backslider Restored New Heart

Bestinia Williams

In 1973, I suffered two heart attacks; one was severe. I was placed on four different types of medication. I began to lose weight and my overall condition was serious.

Last April the Spirit of God began to bring conviction to my heart. I was a backslider in need of restoration. The Lord accepted me back into the fold. Shortly after my restoration, the Lord gave me a new heart. Since then I have not had any medication. I praise God for this ministry of faith. Not only do I have a new heart, but I have also gained 40 pounds.

No More Heart Problem

Wanda Alvarado

The Lord delivered me from Rhuematic heart disease. I was born with Rhuematic fever which damaged my heart. I had three Rhuematic heart attacks. My doctor had placed me on two hundred thousand units of bicillin per month. I had been taking this medication for sixteen years and had become totally dependent on it. Praise God, January, 1978,

Tumor Disappears

Lillie Ruth Dozier

The last night of the City-Wide Camp Meeting last year I was instantly healed of a tumor in my right breast. My breast was sore and sensitive to touch. Even the task of putting on my bra would cause pain. The pain was so severe that it was difficult for me to bathe. This condition was in my body for over two months. Thank God for the power of the Holy Spirit which went through my body like lightening. All the pain and soreness immediately disappeared. The lump was instantaneously dissolved. I praise God that there is no more pain, for I was healed by the power of God.

God delivered me. Since that time I have been off medication. There have been no after effects because I have been completely delivered by the power of the Holy Ghost.

Diabetes

R. L. Drew

On May 14, 1978, the Lord healed me of sugar diabetes. I had entered Veterans Hospital for a toe infection. Upon examination, the doctor discovered that I had sugar. The doctor placed me on a special diet and I had to have insulin daily. Praise God, since the Lord touched me, I have not taken any insulin. Today, I am able to eat whatever I desire. I thank God for His healing power.

Tumor Nerves High Blood

Sis. D. Blunt

Thank God for healing me of a tumor. The doctor informed me that if I didn't have the tumor removed, it would kill me. In addition to the tumor, I had a nervous condition and high blood pressure. The doctor had placed me on medication. I was determined not to undergo surgery for the removal of the tumor. I knew that God was able to deliver me. God is faithful, for on May 26, 1978, God removed the tumor, regulated my pressure, and relieved me of the nervous condition. I've been off medication for six months and I praise God for the victory.

And Deliverance Lasts

Elder Marvin Loadholt

Prior to becoming a part of this ministry, I had been going to the doctor because of chest pains. Following a series of tests including a skin test and an x-ray, it was discovered that there was a spot on my lungs.

My wife had been attending a revival that was conducted by Rev. Johnnie Washington in 1968. She invited me to the meeting and I accepted her invitation.

The first night that I attended the meeting nothing apparently happened to me. The second night my heart was touched by the word of God and I went forward when the alter call was made. Thank God, I was saved, delivered and set free by the power of God.

Two weeks after that memorable night, I returned to the doctor. He could not find anything wrong with me. It has been ten years and I am still healed. God has since called me into the ministry and ordained me to preach the gospel and has given me my own radio broadcast. Thank God for the miracle-working power of the Holy Ghost.

AND YOU SHALL KNOW THE TRUTH

Is There Life After Death?

Sis. Faye L. Carson

You are not the first to have asked this question. In the Old Testament it is recorded that Job asked, "If a man die, shall he live again?" (Job 14:14).

Man instinctively believes in life after death. This can be seen in various records of ancient civilizations. One in particular is the ancient civilization of Egypt. Elaborate preprations of the bodies of the dead were a part of this civilization (embalmment, pyramids, etc.)

However, let us look into the scriptures and see what God has to say regarding life after death. Job responds to his own question by stating that even if the skin worms destroyed him, he would see God in his flesh. (Job 19:26)

The Lord Jesus Christ taught that there would be life after death. His response to the Sadducees who denied that there was a resurrection was, "ye do err, not knowing the Scriptures nor the power of God. But as touching the resurrection of the dead, have ye not read that which was spoken unto you by God saying, I am the God of Abraham, and the God of Isaac, and the God of Jacob? God is not the God of the dead, but of the living." (Matt. 22:29, 31-32)

Jesus also reminded Martha in John 11:25-26, "I am the resurrection and the life: he that believeth in me, though he were dead, yet shall he live. And whosoever liveth and believeth in me shall never die."

It is true that there is life after death. The most important question is where will you spend eternity? Revelations 20:5-6 states that there will be two resurrections -- the resurrection of the just and the resurrection of the wicked dead. Be certain of your destiny by receiving Christ as your personal Saviour.

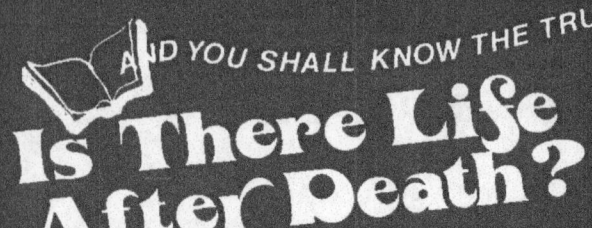

Tabernacle Bible Institute

The Tabernacle Bible Institute will once again open its doors to those who are interested in studying God's word. Don't miss this opportunity to study to show thyself approved unto God, a workman that needeth not to be ashamed, rightly dividing the word of truth. Registration begins Tuesday, September 5, 1978. Courses offered are:

Book of Romans	2 yrs.
Book of Revelation	1 yr.
Christian Workers	1 yrs.
General Bible	2 yrs.
Teachers Training	2 yrs.
Post Graduate	2 yrs.
English	2 yrs.
Reading	

Apostle Johnnie Washington, President & Founder
Elder C. R. Johnson, Dean
Sister Faye Carson, Assistant Dean

IF IT'S ANYTHING LIKE LAST YEAR... *Hallelujah!*

Plan Now **GOLDSBORO, N.C.**
the RALEIGH-DURHAM AREA

"DEEPER LIFE" HOLY GHOST - SUPERNATURAL
CRUSADE • CONVENTION

BEGINNING... AUG 25TH THRU... SEPT 4TH

Evang. Johnnie **WASHINGTON** & Elder **C.R. JOHNSON**
CRUSADE PARTY & CRUSADE CHOIR•••

BUSES LEAVE 11 P.M. FRI. Sept 1 **LABOR DAY** Weekend
FOR RESERVATIONS CALL...(201) 657-4210

Faith & Deliverance BROADCAST

The impact of the Holy Ghost filled message of deliverance as preached by Apostle Washington has stirred the very foundation of the adversary. Men and women everywhere are experiencing real deliverance and are coming to know Jesus Christ as Lord and Master of their lives.

WADO 1280 AM DIAL
8:00-8:30 A.M. .... Sundays
NEW YORK, NEW JERSEY, CONN.

WWDJ 97 AM
6-6:30 PM .... Sundays
NEW YORK, NEW JERSEY, MET. AREA

KAAY 1090 KHZ
11:30-11:45 PM .... Sundays
LITTLE ROCK, ARKANSAS AREA

WOKJ 1550 KHZ
7-7:30 AM .... Sundays
JACKSON, MISSISSIPPI AREA

WDIA 1070 KHZ
10:30-11:00 AM .... Sundays
MEMPHIS, & SOUTHERN, NORTHERN & WESTERN STATES

WANN 1190 RADIO DIAL
11:30-11:45 AM .... Monday through Friday
MARYLAND, (ANNAPOLIS) DELAWARE & VIRGINIA

WWVA 1170 KHZ DIAL
11:45-12:00 Midnight .. Monday through Friday
WHEELING, W. VA. EASTERN SEABOARD

WNCT 1070
8:00-8:30 A.M. .... Sundays
GREENVILLE, N. CAROLINA AREA

WSWN 900 RADIO DIAL
8:45-9:00 A.M. .... Saturdays
BELLE GLADE, FLORIDA AREA

WOKN 102.3 FM DIAL
9-9:30 .... Sundays
GOLDSBORO, NORTH CAROLINA AREA

WOKT 1270 RADIO DIAL
11:30-12:00 Noon .... Saturdays
NORFOLK, VIRGINIA AREA

Tabernacle Fellowship Family

General Headquarters
Jamaica, N.Y.
165-11 Jamaica Ave.

- Goldsboro, N.C.
  South S\locumb St.
  Pastor Lawrence Bogier

- Wallace, N.C.
  Pastor Hattie Carlton

- Laurinburg, N.C.
  320 McGrits Rd
  Pastor Alonzo Legget

- Newark, N.J.
  407 Broad St
  Pastor Clyde Moore

- Norfolk, Va.
  304 E. 25th St.
  Pastor Myrtle M. Terry

- Wilson, N.C.
  616 Lane St

- Rochester, N.Y.
  715 Ave. D
  Pastor Apostle Johnnie Washington
  Asst. Pastor Ida Hamilton
  Pastor H. Fields

- Fort Pierce, Fla.
  Douglas Ct. & Ave D
  Pastor Overa Stevens
  Pastor Harry Gordan

- Smithfield, N.C.

- Baltimore, Md.
  1231-33 E. Biddle St.
  4617 York Rd.
  Pastor Aaron A. Claxton
  Pastor R. Smoot

- Trinidad
  13 Churches
  Headquarters: San Fernando
  Bishop R. B. Ramsahai

TABERNACLE OF PRAYER FOR ALL PEOPLE, INC.
P. O. Box 153
Brooklyn, N. Y. 11233

NON-PROFIT ORG.
U.S. POSTAGE
PAID
PERMIT No. 11576
BROOKLYN, N.Y.

ARE YOU MOVING?

If you are going to move within the next month, please send your name and address, and give your new address and send to our mailing address which is: Tabernacle of Prayer for All People, Inc., P.O. Box 153, Brooklyn, New York 11233 so that you will not miss your next issue of your "CRY ALOUD" magazine.

Thousands have been reached

But in our hands have been placed an even greater task. That is to reach millions before Christ's soon return. Yes! We rejoice as we see the tremendous growth in such a short time and we rejoice again as testimonies from our tent, church, crusade and radio ministries cross our desk. But our hearts are made heavy again as we see so many more that we know we can reach, if given the support.

Today, even right now, as you read these words, ask God what He would have you to do to help us. Obey Him and I know, beyond a shadow of a doubt, that God will bless you abundantly above all you may ask or think. "Prove Me" God declares in Malachi 3:10 "If I will not open the windows of heaven and pour you out a blessing that there shall not be room enough to receive it."

Yours Because We Love Souls

Apostle Johnnie Washington
Apostle Johnnie Washington

I WANT TO BE A TABERNACLE *Torchbearer*

I (we) enclose $.......... to be used as indicated below:

Monthly Volunteer's Pledge Offering .... $........
Gift for the Radio Broadcast Ministry .... $........
Gift for the Deliverance Supernatural Crusades . $........
Deliverance Tent Ministry .... $........
My Faith Tithes Offering .... $........
My Love Offering To Apostle Washington ...... $........

Name _____ (please print) _____
Address _____ Apt. No. _____
City _____ State/ _____ Zip/Postal Code _____

90-07 Merrick Blvd. Jamaica, New York 11432

TABERNACLE *Christian* Book Store

Large Selection Of Bibles   Christian Literature
Sunday School Material   Gospel Records
& Tabernacles Own Tapes
With Apostle Johnny Washington

For Information Call 523-1912

CONSECRATION AND PERSONALITY

Washington was known for his fiery personality. He was strongly against any kind of duplicity. Being single-minded and consistent in all places seemed to be part of the holy life. Yet what drove him the hardest was his profound sense of urgency. All ministry endeavors were pursued intensely and with much fervor—no excuses. Nothing was a sufficient reason not to "work the works of him that sent him." This urgency seems to be informed by his early battles with sickness—including suffering a heart attack at 25 years old. He requested that he not be taken to the hospital but taken home. Here he prayed fervently until the pain subsided. He used his healing to propel him into even greater work of ministry. Tomorrow was promised to no man and thus Apostle Washington was determined to make the most of today for Christ. "They did not seem to be listening to the same clock that was ticking away...I constantly urged my pastors to do more, pray more, fast more, evangelize more, witness more. Saints, I was in a hurry. My time was running out, so much to do Lord, so little time."[17]

Although he was known for his direct and blunt sermons over the pulpit, outside of that he had a softer personality. His love for people was as intense as his rebukes. He was honest and sincere; his refusal to have any double mindedness demanded it. His love for them was the source of his rebukes and correction. Yet beyond this, his staff spoke of his delightful sense of humor. "Pastor was fun to be with and he loved to tell funny stories about things that had happened to him and others in the church. One of his favorite past-times was laughing at the hats worn by some of the sisters in the church."

DEATH AND LEGACY

As the middle of the 1980s drew closer, Apostle Washington's intense fervor for ministry seemed to increase. He showed no signs of slowing down although he was getting older. The church continued to have their regularly scheduled services and he also assumed a leadership role in another branch church in Philadelphia. At the same time, he continued to conduct crusade revivals across the nation, building up the Tabernacle Fellowship. Slowly his health took a toll with mysterious growths on his face. Washington refused to seek medical care or to take a sabbatical. Of it, he said, "There was much love and concern, but I knew that it was misplaced...[It was] advice that conflicts with orders from above" (Pg. 92).

Thankfully, the growths shrunk miraculously, and he recovered. Yet his drive for ministry continued to increase with little to no rest. In 1985, he suffered a stroke that affected his memory, mobility, and motor skills. Apostle Washington continued to function as leader of the church until his physical appearance at their Annual Convention stunned many of his followers and raised concerns about his health. Not long after, he went into a vegetative state from the stroke. His son, Johnnie Jr., moved him to a hospital in California, where he lived so that he could be nearer to him. On April 22, 1986, Apostle Johnnie L. Washington passed away from the complications. His funeral was held in California, where he was also buried. Tabernacle of Prayer in Queens had to hold a memorial service in his honor without the body present, adding to their burden of grief. The church continued under the leadership of Apostle Ira Davidson and now, Bishop Ronny Davis.

The legacy of Apostle Johnnie L. Washington is one of unflinching compromise, discipline, demonstration, and dedication to the Scriptures. Tabernacle of Prayer took the movement to another level by settling it into the local church. Apostle Washington combined the mantles of evangelistic and pastoral ministry in order to double his impact in

Brooklyn but also in the entire nation. His ministry met the harsh social climate of the 1980s riddled with drugs, political unrest, crime, and disease with an equally magnetic "Word of God." Tabernacle's thorough commitment to structure, education, and stewardship refined the Deliverance movement, earning it a position in the local church for generations to come.

---

1 Washington, Johnnie and Cynthia Hedgepeth. Lord Why Me: The Making of an Apostle. Queens, NY: Tabernacle of Prayer Publishing. Pg. 34.

2 Washington and Hedgepeth. Lord Why Me, 49.

3 Ibid, 53.

4 Ibid, 81.

5 Larry J. McKinney. "The Fundamentalist Bible School as an Outgrowth of the Changing Patterns of Protestant Revivalism, 1882-1920", Religious Education: The Official Journal of the Religious Education Association, 84:1, 589-605. Pg. 594.

6 Washington and Hedgepeth. Lord Why Me, pg. 72.

7 Murray, James. "Behind the Scenes at Queens' Loew's Valencia, once the most successful Wonder Theatre in NYC." 6sqft, Nov. 6, 2018. Accessed April 17, 2021. https://www.6sqft.com/behind-the-scenes-at-queens-loews-valencia-once-the-most-successful-wonder-theatre-in-nyc/.

8 Gray, Christopher, "Streetscapes: Jamaica's Valencia Theater; A Success Story Masks a Landmarks Law Quirk." The New York Times. April 15, 1990. Accessed April 17, 2021.

9 Synan, The Century of the Holy Spirit, Pg. 286.

10 JesusSaves2341, "Precious Memories: Tribute to Apostle Washington," YouTube video, 7:04, March 13, 2010, https://www.youtube.com/watch?v=OoxFheNor34.

11 Washington and Hedgepeth. Lord Why Me, Pg. 81.

12 JesusSaves2341, "Precious Memories: Tribute to Apostle Washington."

13 Washington and Hedgepeth. Lord, Why Me, Pg. 98.

14 Samuel Guillame, Interview with the author, January 6, 2021.

15 Archbishop Bernard Jordan, Interview with the author, Power of Prophecy, March 17, 2021.

16 Cry Aloud, Vol. 1, No. 1, 1978. Periodical.

17 Washington and Hedgepeth. Lord Why Me?, pg. 81.

PROPHET MOSLEY

If apostle is the most debated office in the church, prophecy is perhaps the most debated spiritual gift. The discussion on prophecy leads to questions such as: Does God still speak today? Does prophecy mean that the canon of Scripture is still open? Are prophets equal to the divinely inspired writers of the Scriptures?

At the time of this writing there are thousands of books, articles, and videos seeking to answer these questions about prophecy. But in our church, and in the Pentecostal tradition, nothing answers critics like a personal experience. The black church has watched the prophetic evolve from a spontaneous manifestation in Azusa Street to an embraced spiritual gift and office with its own systems in place. At the center of the development of the prophetic movement, especially in the black church, is a man named Brian Jefferson Mosley or, as he is more affectionately known, "Prophet Mosley." When Prophet Mosley's ministry came forth in the 1970s and 80s, the title "Prophet" was not common. Bill Hamon wrote, "The office of the prophet was still the occasional one. Even those who received and taught that there were prophets in the Church did not have the faith and freedom to identify a man as such.

They would introduce a minister as 'Evangelist.'[3]

What Mosley brought to the body of Christ was unlike anything they had experienced before. Mosley's ministry demonstrated the manifestation of all spiritual gifts with an unmatched consistency in delivery, especially in giving a word of knowledge, a word of wisdom, and prophecy. This earned him the title, "Prophet."

EARLY LIFE AND BEGINNINGS

Brian Jefferson Mosley was born July 30th in New Haven, Connecticut. Not much is known of his birth parents. He was adopted by an older woman when he was still a small child. From an early age, Mosley had a passion for ministry and preaching.

Mosley was raised in the Congregational Church. But at 13, he experienced conversion in a Baptist church. Nonetheless, Mosley found himself intrigued by something called "Baptism in the Holy Ghost." He decided to seek this experience. He attended a local Church of God in Christ where he received this blessing and spoke with tongues. He then learned of "Baptism in Jesus' name" from a local Oneness church, which differed from his Baptist traditions on Baptism. Young Brian Mosley was anything but a church sectarian. He never confined himself to a particular denomination or church. He was raised in a Congregational church. A friend of his invited him to a Baptist church where he experienced conversion. But he recalls being intrigued by local Pentecostal churches where people spoke with tongues and danced before the Lord. "I didn't think of differentiating or dismissing churches. I never went in saying, 'This church doesn't…' Instead, my attitude was always 'How do they experience the presence of God here?' Some people considered it to be church hopping, but I just really loved God and my relationship with Him kept me afloat."[1] Mosley's ecumenical approach to the Holy Spirit would prove valuable to him in his future ministry.

Eventually, he attended the Church of God in Christ where he received the Baptism in the Holy Ghost, much to his mother's dismay. Young Mosley was forbidden to attend meetings with the "Holy Rollers" and had to make do with what he had. But instead of giving up altogether, he made everywhere he went his pulpit. He would minister to his classmates in school, friends, and whomever he could. As a result, he cannot pinpoint when he specifically realized he was called to ministry. "I was always ministering to people. So I can't pinpoint a specific time of day when I knew. I sort of always knew God had something for me to do."[2] From the onset, Mosley displayed a significant interest in people's behavior and actions. He recalls "The first time I went to tarry service, I couldn't even focus on praying for myself because I was so enamored with the other young people crying out to God, praying and seeking God."[3] Eventually this produced a ministry of prayer and intercession for others. He would find himself praying fervently for others as if for his own self. Eventually this intense intercession would be followed up with what he called "great impressions." After praying for people, he would feel the burning need to share something with them. He would find himself telling them what would happen and began watching his words come to pass. Although he didn't know the specific name for it then, it was the manifestation of prophecy.

Not much was known of the gift of prophecy at that time. "The primary people that flowed in that type of gift were women and even then, they didn't have titles for it," said Dr. Mosley. "Men preached often, but they didn't really get deep into prayer and definitely not the prophetic. People like Bishop C.H. Mason were rare for his time."[4] Bishop Mason, the founder of Church of God in Christ, was known for his deep Pentecostal spirituality. But part of his popularity was the scarcity of this type of spiritual gifting as a man. Although he had many women who followed suit in prayer, many men did not.

Young Mosley was eventually licensed and ordained into ministry and began ministering in youth revivals, services and conferences as a teenager in Connecticut.

MINISTRY AND DEVELOPMENT

Young Evangelist Mosley had services throughout Connecticut in the mid-1970s, slowly stirring his popularity. But one invitation would increase the momentum of his ministry for good. He ministered at a predominantly Spanish church called Iglesia Cristiana Buen Pastor, translated as Good Shepherd Christian Church, and revival broke out. The house was jam packed as he went forth ministering to the people. This engagement testified to the legitimacy of his gifting as many of these people who didn't speak English experienced the anointing. "It was the same power that was in the black Church. The Holy Ghost knows no barriers!"[5]

These meetings increased his popularity and caused him to develop a following of supporters throughout the state. Each revival meeting increased his followership, soon making it difficult to have sufficient space anywhere. "One thing about my meetings," Mosley said, "people were gonna get saved!" Although Mosley was gifted prophetically, he had a strong burden for evangelism.

Nonetheless, the signature of his meetings was that there was no signature. "Every night was different. You never knew what would happen," Mosley reminisced. Prophet Mosley's refusal to confine himself to a particular gift or manifestation was his key to being used by God freely. "We flowed in the 9 gifts of the Spirit. Whatever God wanted to do I was totally open to it."

With that, his meetings were largely spontaneous and unpredictable. One of the main manifestations in his meeting was being "slain in the Spirit" or "falling out" in the Spirit. "That particular thing caused significant controversy for me because people were always falling out," said Mosley.[6]

Being slain in the Spirit is a common manifestation in Pentecostal churches, especially in revival meetings. Word of faith teacher Kenneth Hagin once explained, "When the natural [body] comes into contact with the supernatural—something has to give."[7] Although being slain in the Spirit was not uncommon in Pentecostal meetings, it was usually prompted by the laying on of hands. However, in Mosley's meetings, sections of people would often experience being slain in the Spirit and often without anyone touching them. Bishop J.C. White attended his revival in Brooklyn and recalled, "I was sitting in the balcony and he saw me up there. He threw a handkerchief into the balcony, it expanded and when I caught it, the entire balcony was slain in the Spirit. "Most preachers would wear the black minister's cape after they finished ministering to keep them warm," recalled Archbishop E. Bernard Jordan. "Prophet Mosley would come out the door with the cape on before he ministered and then wave it over people, they would be slain in the Spirit. He would lay it on people for healing. He was radical!"[8]

Although many testified positively of this experience, many opponents spoke critically of Mosley's meetings. Many critics felt that Mosley's meetings targeted poor people because of their ignorance. However, most of them would be insulted at the idea that being poor made them ignorant, unlearned, and prey to deception. Mosley stated that his meetings attracted those from all economic classes. Others said it was simply a placebo effect and that those people went to those meetings to escape a painful reality and returned to it afterward. However, the testimonies that followed and still remain to this day from meetings in the 1980s counter that idea. Criticism did not deter him. For Mosley, the number of people that were slain under the power testified to the atmosphere: "When people came into my meetings, it was prayed up. People would pray all before the service and during. You don't really find things like that these days. People don't pray. That was what set the room."[9]

Still, his most known asset was his prophetic gifting. Mosley ministered heavily under "word of knowledge" and "prophecy." In Pentecostal belief, word of knowledge is the revealing of facts about a person by the Holy Spirit. People that function in this gift often point to the example of the Holy Spirit's specificity with Peter and Cornelius in Acts 10:19-23 and Ananias with Saul in Acts 9:10-12. Mosley would often call out people by name and identify places and other facts without knowing those people personally. This type of manifestation was also largely uncommon. Prophecies often came in "tongues and interpretation" and often addressed sin, the second coming, or someone's need for deliverance. Bishop E. Bernard Jordan, a contemporary prophetic voice, explained,

"We prophesy according to the proportion of our faith. In Pentecostal belief there are three works of grace: salvation, sanctification, and baptism in the Holy Ghost. Since Azusa Street and into the 1970s, the Pentecostal church was amidst that second grace: sanctification. So, all you heard was 'Be Holy!' But eventually it evolved."[10]

The evolution of prophecy seems to be linked with the Charismatic Renewal in the 1960s and 70s where spiritual gifts became present in otherwise non-Pentecostal churches. It is during this time that the work of the Spirit was beginning to shift. Author Bill Hamon explained "[At that time] The Holy Spirit was striving to bring the Body of Christ to a new faith level and a greater revelation of truth so that the material things needed could be brought in to communicate the gospel and prosper the Church."[11] Naturally, the genre of prophetic words began to shift as well from broad to personal and from mystical to practical.

Mosley's seamless ability to flow in this style of prophetic gift was undeniable. It caused his popularity to increase regionally, nationally, and internationally. But his itinerant ministry was not confined just to ministry invitations for churches. Evangelist Mosley also ran tent revivals and crusades around the country. The tent meetings were just as fiery as his in-church services. Evangelist Mosley's meetings combined driving music, holy dancing, direct preaching, and ministry through the laying on of hands. "I always preferred being in the tent because that was the Tabernacle in the Bible," Mosley stated. Mosley referenced the Tabernacle in the wilderness that the Children of Israel traveled with in Exodus 25 that housed the presence of the Lord. For Mosley, his tent was a continuation of that Tabernacle where the presence of God would dwell.

Most poignant though, is the fact that Mosley did not take his revival meetings to areas considered "safe" by other white evangelists. Revivals were unflinchingly run in Brownsville, Camden, Newburgh, Bridgeport, Baltimore, and especially in Newark, New Jersey. All these cities were considered some of the most dangerous on the East coast and the subject of frequent news reports about shooting, looting, murder, and so on.

For Mosley, this was no big deal. "I simply went wherever the Lord would send me," Mosley reasoned. However, the location of the meetings was a message within itself. The presence of the tent in the middle of the "hood" signified a faith that was unafraid of the harsh realities that surrounded people and boldly countered the violence, drugs, and poverty with the Gospel message.

The ecstatic sounds of revival fit snugly into the bustling, lively streets of these urban communities. But interestingly enough, to the mainstream church culture, tent revivals were considered obsolete after the 1960s. "By the 1960s, society was going through an upheaval and church revivals stopped drawing crowds. Evangelists found new, larger audiences by preaching on television, and air-conditioned churches proved more appealing than hot, dusty tents."[12]

In the black Pentecostal church however, the 1980s were a peak for evangelistic ministries like those of Prophet Mosley and Apostle Johnnie Washington who used this as a time to counter the ungodly culture of the "streets." Refusing to be confined, Mosley's ministry spanned from the local concrete streets to the palaces of the Motherland. In 1982, Prophet Brian Mosley was invited to Swaziland in southern Africa to run crusades and preach the Gospel. Yet he found himself amidst a royal family battle. While there, he prophesied to a young teenager and anointed him to be King.[13] His father, King Sobuza II, had just passed away and the country had organized a special regency to rule the country. The Prince was not set to be King until he turned 21. There was also a power struggle within the royal family for rulership. "I had all kinds of people in the royal family coming to me by night asking me to prophesy this one or that one as the next ruler. But I can't go against what God showed me. I saw Mswati as the next King."[14] When Young King Mswati visited his meeting, Prophet Mosley prophesied his kingship and anointed him for such immediately. He was crowned king in 1986 at the age of 18, the youngest Monarch in the Nation's history and still reigning to this day.[15]

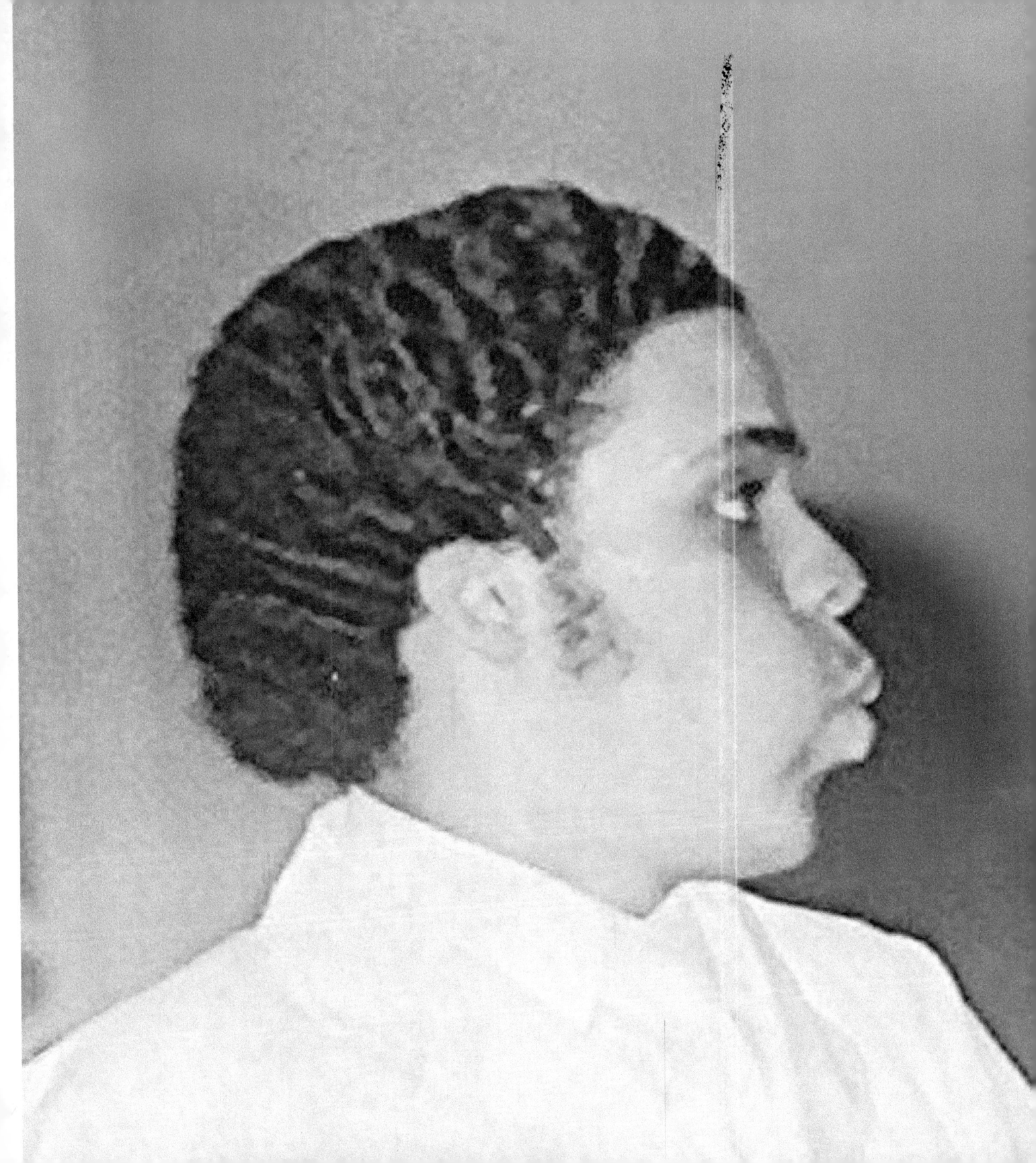

Greater Bethlehem Healing Temple

(Original Pentecostal Church Body, Inc.)

286 South 7th Street
at South Orange Avenue
Newark, New Jersey

Moshe Ben Yisrael

Prophet B. Jefferson Mosley
Founder/General Overseer

A happy welcome to all of you. The Greater Bethlehem Healing Temple family considers it an honor and privlege to have you worship with us and sincerely hopes that you get a blessing from the service. We trust that you will feel at home and will return real soon.

GBHT

ORDER OF SERVICE

Elder Reynold McZorn .... Presiding Elder

10:00 a.m.
SABBATH SCHOOL

12:00 noon
HIGH SACRED SERVICE

Prayer and Scripture .... Around the Altar
Organ Prelude ....
Call to Worship .... Evangelist Pauline Moore
Hymn .... No. 27 "The Church's One Foundation"
Responsive Reading .... Exodus 20:1-17
James 2:8-13
St. Matthew 22:36-40
Hymn .... No. 57 "No One Ever Cared Like Jesus"
Missionary Offering .... Missionary Louise Ginn
Tithing Service .... Mal. 3:7-12
Organ - The Church's One Foundation
Offertory Prayer .... alternate
Matt: 6:9-13
Hymn .... No. 129 "Yield Not To Temptation"
Sermon .... Prophet B. Jefferson Mosley
Presiding Overseer and Chief Apostle
Invitation to Discipleship
Doxology
Benediction

4:00 p.m.
MEN IN CHARGE

Prayer and Scripture .... Around the Altar
Call to Worship .... Men's Department
"But the hour is coming, and now is, when the worshippers will worship the Father in Spirit and Truth, for such the Father seeks to worship Him. God is a Spirit, and those who worship Him must worship Him in Spirit and in Truth."
Consecration Offering .... Evangelist Pauline Moore
Selection ....
Speakers ....

Invitation to Discipleship ....
General Offering .... Finance Committee
Benediction ....

OCTOBER 28, 1989

Let every person render to governing authorities. Romans 13:A

Sunday, 5:00 p.m. .... Broadcast Service
Tuesday, 7:00 p.m. .... Men's Prayer
Tuesday, 7:00 p.m. .... Bible Class
Conducted by Pastor Mosley
Friday, 6:00 p.m. .... Holy Ghost Rally

Sabbath School: Every Saturday morning at 10:00 a.m. for adults, youth and children. We encourage visitors to join us in discovering the knowledge and truth of Our Lord and Savior Jesus Christ.

ANNOUNCEMENTS

All announcements must be in the office by Sunday of each week if you would like them to appear in the Saturday morning bulletin.

Charitable Love: If you can't visit the sick, send a card. A cheery card could brighten their day. If you miss the person that usually sits next to you, call and encourage them.

We then that are strong ought to bear the infirmities of the weak, and not to please ourselves.
ROMANS 15:1

PASTOR'S AIDES MEETING
Sunday, October 29, 1989
4:00 p.m.

MEETING
ALL AUXILIARY HEADS
Monday, October 30, 1989
Time to be announced

FOOD BANK Please bring in your canned goods to help the needy!

Grace, Mercy and Peace
From God the Father and Christ Jesus our Lord

Remembering the words of our Lord to Peter in St. John 21:15-18, "Feed My Lambs . . . Feed My Sheep . . . Feed My Sheep" and realizing that we are living in the day when men and women will not endure sound doctrine, I endeavor, through the unction and inspiration of the Holy Ghost, to, embark upon the most difficult task of leading God's people unto the perfect knowledge of the oneness of that great God, Elohim, our Savior in the person of Jesus Christ. Not only am I convinced, but also convicted that God is requiring PURE HOLINESS from His people in these last days and times, as well as the preaching of the unadulterated PENTECOSTAL message that the Apostles preached and taught among the people of their day, deplete of all pagan CUSTOMS and unscriptual religious HOLIDAYS. Yes, He is Calling for His people to come out of "Babylon", that great harlot.

Prophet B. Jefferson Mosley

Chief Apostle and General Overseer

CHURCH PHONE: 485-2038

YOU ARE INVITED TO WORSHIP WITH US:

Broadcast Service	Sunday, 5:00 p.m.
Men's Prayer	Tuesday, 7:00 p.m.
Bible Class	Tuesday, 7:00 p.m.
Holy Ghost Rally	Friday, 6:00 p.m.
Sabbath School	Saturday, 10:00 a.m.
Sabbath Morning Worship	Saturday, 12:00 p.m.
Sabbath Afternoon Worship	Saturday, 4:00 p.m.

A happy welcome to all of you. The Greater Bethlehem Healing Temple family considers it an honor and privlege to have you worship with us and sincerely hopes that you get a blessing from the service. We trust that you will feel at home and will return real soon.

GBHT

ORDER OF SERVICE

Elder Reynold McZorn .... Presiding Elder

10:00 a.m.
SABBATH SCHOOL

12:00 noon
HIGH SACRED SERVICE

Prayer and Scripture .... Around the Altar
Organ Prelude ....
Call to Worship .... Evangelist Pauline Moore
Hymn .... No. 27 "The Church's One Foundation"
Responsive Reading .... Exodus 20:1-17
                                                    James 2:8-13
                                                    St. Matthew 22:36-40
Hymn .... No. 57 "No One Ever Cared Like Jesus"
Missionary Offering .... Missionary Louise Ginn
Tithing Service .... Mal. 3:7-12
Organ - The Church's One Foundation
Offertory Prayer .... alternate
                                                    Matt: 6:9-13
Hymn .... No. 129 "Yield Not To Temptation"
Sermon .... Prophet B. Jefferson Mosley
                                Presiding Overseer and Chief Apostle

Invitation to Discipleship
Doxology
Benediction

4:00 p.m.
MEN IN CHARGE

Prayer and Scripture .... Around the Altar
Call to Worship .... Men's Department
"But the hour is coming, and now is, when the worshippers will worship the Father in Spirit and Truth, for such the Father seeks to worship Him. God is a Spirit, and those who worship Him must worship Him in Spirit and in Truth."
Consecration Offering .... Evangelist Pauline Moore
Selection ....
Speakers ....

Invitation to Discipleship ....
General Offering .... Finance Committee
Benediction ....

PERSONALITY AND CONSECRATION

Prophet Mosley's revivals were so popular, they became a subject of a documentary by PBS called "Prophet." The documentary chronicled the third week of his long-running tent meeting in Newark, New Jersey in 1988. Mosley pitched his tent in the Central Ward neighborhood of Newark and held revival consisting of "head-dunking baptisms" and "trembling parishioners" as Albert Parisi described it.[16]

The meeting's impact was featured in a New York Times article. In it, PBS Senior Correspondent Sandra King stated, "In a way, you can't dismiss him as a fraud just from the passion he shows... and whether he works through mass hypnosis or sheer emotion, he reaches people."[17] Mosley attributes his impact to his love for people. "Many times, the people were looking to me. But they didn't know I was looking to them. I remember there was this one deacon who I could never see after a meeting without us both quickening and going up speaking in tongues. People would call me strange or eclectic for loving that but I loved those moments. They gave me strength!" Mosley's driving love for people proved to be indispensable in his ministry.

In the documentary, Mosley is seen laying hands on people for them to receive "healing and deliverance," with many of those people being slain in the spirit. Videos of Mosley ministering are cut away with a skeptical doctor refuting his actions as emotional or a placebo effect.

One action in particular is when he grabs a young sickly child by the arm and lays hands on her, a move that is still criticized by YouTube commenters to this day. And continued to be until a young lady commented on the YouTube video claiming, "I'm the baby that he grabbed in that video. Wow, 30 years later!"[18] Although the methods may be criticized, Mosley felt validated by the testimonies that followed. It was not uncommon for meeting attendants to pass tumors in the restroom during service, for lumps to disappear, and drug addictions to be broken. One attendant recalled they were under the power of God so strongly that they no longer needed their glasses.

Mosley was known for wearing all white when ministering and sometimes all black. "Saints wore white for special occasions, and I did the same thing when I ministered. I also wanted to look differently than everyone else. I wasn't a robe guy, but I liked to stand out," Mosley explained.[19] His donning of all white and use of all black conveyed a message of seriousness, piety, and solemness. Ironically, his smoothed back hair, light skin complexion, and glowing eyes made many people compare him to the Artist Formerly Known as Prince.

Mosley's transcendent demeanor added to the awe-striking atmosphere of his meetings. Elder Michael Jackson served as a traveling armorbearer (ministry assistant) with Dr. Mosley. He recalled his encounters with Mosley's meetings. "People were terrified of him. He had a solemn, serious look to him. You didn't want to look him in the eyes. You would feel all the discipline he walked in when he looked at you."[20] Another story recalled that a meeting detractor came into the service swearing, fuming with anger and upon Mosley making eye contact with him he fell flat on his back. When he came back to consciousness, he confessed Christ and gave his heart to the Lord.[21] Jackson described Mosley walking into his meetings as a "burning match walking into a gas station." Upon entry, the congregation would burn with the intense passion of Pentecost, subject to the spontaneous direction of "The Spirit." "It wasn't just the people being overwhelmed. I can remember the hand of the Lord being so heavy on Mosley that he had to be carried out of the service himself," Jackson said.

Prophet Mosley pastored the Greater Bethlehem Healing Temple for 12 years in Newark. He was also the general overseer and bishop of the original Pentecostal churches. By the time he began pastoring, Mosley had become a Sabbath Keeper. Sabbath Keepers are Messianic Jews that embrace Pentecostal spirituality. They affirm the keeping of the law, including dietary law, and observe the Sabbath day as a day of holy worship. His Newark church centralized his impact in the Tri-State area and beyond. By this time, Mosley had also developed a team of equally gifted and consecrated people. Many of them were gifted as prophets as well. He also attracted other aspiring evangelists and prophets everywhere he ministered.

Prophet Mosley's credibility of his gift allowed him to be the first to revive the Biblical concept of "School of the Prophets." The school was based on the biblical precedents of 1 Samuel 19:18-24 and Elijah's school in 2 Kings 2-3. Here, students would learn how to hear from God and give prophetic words with emphasis on accuracy and protocol. Classes were held at Essex County College. "I started the school because there was a need for people to understand ministry. Ministry is not a place where you make a living, it's a place where you give your life. We didn't really have resources then but I wanted people to understand ministry."²² Classes were not always focused on supernatural protocol and phenomena. Instead, Mosley stated, "I taught people how to serve. I didn't focus heavily on a curriculum. I taught service and compassion. Sure, we profiled people like Smith Wigglesworth and William Branham, but it is about serving God's people."

After 12 years of pastoral ministry, Prophet Mosley returned to full-time itinerant ministry where he continues to function to this day. "To be honest with you," Mosley reasoned, "I don't believe anyone should pastor beyond 12 years. You never want to stay anywhere too long and lose your effectiveness. Preachers tend to build dynasties instead of ministry. It's difficult for any succession to come from that and after 12 years you have a whole new group of people and a new generation."²³ The demands of global ministry often conflicted with his pastoring. Mosley believed he had taken his congregation as far as he could take them. He continued to minister around the country and the world as he felt led.

LEGACY

Prophet Brian Mosley is different from those listed in this book because he is a living legend. He has outlived many of his ministry contemporaries, a truth that he is grateful for and also humbled by. Prophet Mosley continues to minister in churches across the nation and is regarded as a "Pentecostal diplomat" for his adaptability in all environments while retaining his spiritual authenticity.

Prophet Mosley's impact can hardly be measured as he continues to make strides that will affect generations to come. In his life, he has overcome obstacles of toxic masculinity that blocked men from embracing prophetic spirituality. Prophet Mosley's dynamic ministry was a powerful challenge to the lack of spiritual sensitivity and emotional expression that was often presumed of black men in church. The spontaneity of Mosley's revival meetings broke the limits off engaging the presence of the Lord. He narrowed the scope of the prophetic revealing the specificity of God toward people and personalizing an otherwise ambiguous spiritual walk. And he established the first order and protocol to create structure and residence for the free-flowing prophetic gift.

---

1 Brian Mosley, Interview with the author, March 25, 2021.

2 Ibid.

3 Brian Mosley, Interview with the author, March 17, 2021.

4 Ibid.

5 Mosley, Interview with the author, March 17, 2021.

6 Ibid.

7 Hagin, Kenneth. Why Do People Fall Under the Power (Broken Arrow, OK: Rhema Publishing, 1981), Page 3.

8 Jordan, Bernard Power of Prophecy Interview.

9 Mosley, Interview with the author, March 25, 2021.

10 Jordan, Interview on Power of Prophecy, March 17, 2021.

11 Hamon, Bill. Apostles, Prophets and the Coming Move of God. Shippensburg, PA: Destiny Image, 1997, Page 132.

12 Sorensen, Karen, "Faith: The Rise and Fall of Tent Revival Services," Taunton Daily Gazette, June 16, 2010, https://www.tauntongazette.com/article/20100616/NEWS/306169952.

13 Nkambule, Mfanukhona, "King Warned of a Coup: Have No Fear Your Majesty," Times of Swaziland, October 23, 2011.

14 Brian Mosley, Interview with the author, March 19, 2021.

15 King Mswati, Encyclopedia Brittanica, April 15, 2021.

16 Parisi, Albert "TV: Under the Revival Tent," The New York Times, December 25, 1988, online. https://www.nytimes.com/1988/12/25/nyregion/tv-under-the-revival-tent.html.

17 Ibid.

18 BusinessProphet, "The Authenticity of Prophet Brian Jefferson Mosley © 1980s," YouTube Video, Dec. 6, 2007, 5:46, https://www.youtube.com/watch?v=IE-ItVZLqXHw&lc=Ugw__a0JdkyJq-f6ASd4AaABAg.

19 Interview with the author, March 19, 2021.

20 Michael Jackson, Interview with the author, March 25, 2021.

21 Interview with the author, March 25, 2021.

22 Interview with the author, March 25, 2021.

23 Ibid.

Lord Why Me? page 103.
Lord Why Me? Page 114.

Hamon, Bill Apostles, Prophets and the coming Move of God, page 87

EPILOGUE

At the time of this writing, we are witnessing the coming forth of many ministry gifts. I am reminded of when Moses desired that "all were prophets and that the Lord would place his Spirit on them" (Numbers 11:29). This desire was fulfilled on the Day of Pentecost and continues to come to pass from generation to generation. While many people desire to flow in the supernatural, these men of God used demonstration of miracles and healings solely to evangelize the unsaved. My greatest desire is to see that evangelistic passion return to the Church. May we be pushed from the comfort of church pasture to the plenteous harvest. The world's population has significantly increased, and people are in need of the Gospel. Jesus commanded us "The harvest truly is plenteous but the labourers are few. Pray ye therefore the Lord of the harvest to send laborers forth into the harvest (Matthew 9:38, KJV). Wherever there is plenty, there will be those with the wrong intent. There are many who are not sincere, unbiblical and false. But there are just as many who are sincere, legitimate and committed to the work of the Lord.

May we all learn from the successes and mistakes of the generations before us. May God turn our hearts toward one another so that the hearts of the sons and daughters are not hardened to the voices of the mothers and fathers. May God turns their hearts in the same manner (Malachi 4:6). The turning of the heart requires vulnerability and openness. There is nothing new under the sun. Many people in our generation can be saved from pain by seeing the wounds of survivors.

Most of all, may we never be caught on personality. May we avoid the idolatry of worshipping ministry figures and actively resist chasing popularity. Instead may we only seek to worship the God of our Fathers.